Mark McGowan

Violence Risk Assessment in Schools

Exploring the Predictive Validity of the Structured Professional Judgment Model

VDM Verlag Dr. Müller

Imprint

Bibliographic information by the German National Library: The German National Library lists this publication at the German National Bibliography; detailed bibliographic information is available on the Internet at http://dnb.d-nb.de.

Any brand names and product names mentioned in this book are subject to trademark, brand or patent protection and are trademarks or registered trademarks of their respective holders. The use of brand names, product names, common names, trade names, product descriptions etc. even without a particular marking in this works is in no way to be construed to mean that such names may be regarded as unrestricted in respect of trademark and brand protection legislation and could thus be used by anyone.

Cover image: www.purestockx.com

Published 2008 Saarbrücken

Publisher:
VDM Verlag Dr. Müller Aktiengesellschaft & Co. KG , Dudweiler Landstr. 125 a,
66123 Saarbrücken, Germany,
Phone +49 681 9100-698, Fax +49 681 9100-988,
Email: info@vdm-verlag.de

Produced in Germany by:
Reha GmbH, Dudweilerstrasse 72, D-66111 Saarbrücken
Schaltungsdienst Lange o.H.G., Zehrensdorfer Str. 11, 12277 Berlin, Germany
Books on Demand GmbH, Gutenbergring 53, 22848 Norderstedt, Germany

Impressum

Bibliografische Information der Deutschen Nationalbibliothek: Die Deutsche Nationalbibliothek verzeichnet diese Publikation in der Deutschen Nationalbibliografie; detaillierte bibliografische Daten sind im Internet über http://dnb.d-nb.de abrufbar.

Alle in diesem Buch genannten Marken und Produktnamen unterliegen warenzeichen-, marken- oder patentrechtlichem Schutz bzw. sind Warenzeichen oder eingetragene Warenzeichen der jeweiligen Inhaber. Die Wiedergabe von Marken, Produktnamen, Gebrauchsnamen, Handelsnamen, Warenbezeichnungen u.s.w. in diesem Werk berechtigt auch ohne besondere Kennzeichnung nicht zu der Annahme, dass solche Namen im Sinne der Warenzeichen- und Markenschutzgesetzgebung als frei zu betrachten wären und daher von jedermann benutzt werden dürften.

Coverbild: www.purestockx.com

Erscheinungsjahr: 2008
Erscheinungsort: Saarbrücken

Verlag: VDM Verlag Dr. Müller Aktiengesellschaft & Co. KG , Dudweiler Landstr. 125 a,
D- 66123 Saarbrücken,
Telefon +49 681 9100-698, Telefax +49 681 9100-988,
Email: info@vdm-verlag.de

Herstellung in Deutschland:
Schaltungsdienst Lange o.H.G., Zehrensdorfer Str. 11, D-12277 Berlin
Books on Demand GmbH, Gutenbergring 53, D-22848 Norderstedt
Reha GmbH, Dudweilerstrasse 72, D-66111 Saarbrücken

ISBN: 978-3-639-01054-1

On April 28, 2000, the U.S. Department of Education and Department of Justice developed guidelines to assist educational agencies in addressing the problem of school violence. The report, *Safeguarding Our Children: An Action Guide*, is a continuation of a collaboration that began with the development and dissemination of the 1998 *Early Warning, Timely Response: A Guide To Safe Schools*. Stressing the importance of evidence based practices, these guidelines are intended to assist schools in the development of school violence prevention plans. This report provides a framework or model for implementing violence prevention plans. The model consists of three tiers beginning with a school wide foundation for all children that include strategies for supporting positive discipline, academic success and mental and emotional wellness. The second tier of the model establishes early intervention services for children identified as those who demonstrate risk for future violence. The third tier of the model culminates in the provision of intensive and collaborative interventions intended for a select few, high need children. Essential to the implementation of this process is the means to identify those students who require intervention as well as their specific areas of need.

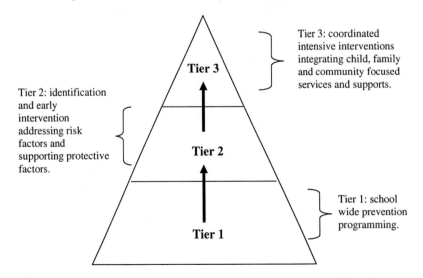

Tier 3: coordinated intensive interventions integrating child, family and community focused services and supports.

Tier 2: identification and early intervention addressing risk factors and supporting protective factors.

Tier 1: school wide prevention programming.

This book builds upon the current developments in violence risk assessment that offer a valid and reliable means for distinguishing between violent and non-violent youth in educational settings. The potential benefits of including a formalized assessment process within the context of broader school safety plans are promising due to the opportunity to identify specific areas of need that may be amenable to intervention intended to reduce risk and build student competencies. Within a comprehensive exploration of evidenced based practices for assessing violence risk, the Structured Professional Judgment model was chosen based upon its flexibility and integration of both clinical and actuarial methodologies. After review of available instruments, the Structured Assessment of Violence Risk in Youth (SAVRY) was chosen as an established assessment instrument that has been validated for use with adolescent populations in both juvenile justice and community mental health settings. This model was applied to assessments conducted with a sample of 87 adolescents enrolled in an alternative educational placement.

The short range goal of this work is to establish a starting point for continued discussion exploring the potential benefits of violence risk assessment as a practical tool within the broader context of school safety plans. The longer range implications include incorporating validated methods that may improve decision making, guide intervention efforts, and enhance treatment efficacy for behaviorally challenged students and their families. The realization of these possibilities will require continued collaboration between researchers, practitioners, and trainers to integrate the available knowledge concerning delinquency, crime, and violence from related fields into the evidenced based practices and treatments utilized by the educational programs serving our children.

- *M. R. M.*

TABLE OF CONTENTS

LIST OF TABLES

LIST OF FIGURES

DEDICATION

To my son, Connor Raymond McGowan.

Chapter 1

Introduction

Faced with the recurring tragedies of school shootings within our nation's educational institutions, public concern regarding violence in our schools has become an area of heightened awareness for educational professionals (Small & Dressler-Tetrick, 2001; Vossekuil, Fein, Reddy, Borum, & Modzeleski, 2002). However, contrary to current public perception, the national statistical trends continue to suggest that schools are safe places, with the base rate for violence in schools demonstrating a consistent decline since 1993 (DeVoe et al., 2003; Snyder, 2004). Similarly, the National Center for Educational Statistics (NCES) in 2003 reported that youth between the ages of 5 and 19 were at least 70 times more likely to be murdered outside the school environment (DeVoe et al.). Initial conclusions drawn from these data would suggest that current concerns surrounding violence within our nation's schools might be ill founded. However, in the year 2003 alone, students ages 12 through 18 were victims of about 150,000 violent crimes at school, a definition that only considers incidences of rape, sexual assault, robbery, and aggravated assault. Further, if the definition of violence is broadened to include incidences of simple assault, the prevalence rates for violence in our nation's schools increases to 740,000 incidences in 2003 (DeVoe, Peter, Noonan, Snyder, & Baum, 2005). When considering the current prevalence rates within a given academic year, these statistics continue to underscore the need to actively address this issue in our schools. Taken together, the conclusions drawn from consideration of these statistics suggest that although the prevalence rates, also referred to as base rates, are relatively low for any given student considering factors such as time or setting; the relative cost of these behaviors on individuals, institutions, and the general public is high. One need only reflect on the incidences of mass murder in our schools to grasp the magnitude of this phenomenon.

Furthermore, in view of the public opinion surrounding the issue of violence in schools, it is reasonable to conclude that these current concerns may relate more to the public's tolerance levels for the relative cost of these behaviors than to the frequency of their occurrence in the general population of students within our schools. One of the primary challenges posed by this problem is encapsulated within the question of whether our educational institutions effectively address a behavioral problem that seems to occur at varying rates in the general population over time. In order to answer this question, it will be important to first consider past practices and current trends for managing school violence within the field of education to date.

Educational professionals' efforts to address school violence have been longstanding. In 1994, an issue of *School Psychology Review*, a publication of the National Association of School Psychologists, dedicated a mini-series to the issue of school violence that advocated for advancement in both research and practice (Furlong & Morrison, 1994). This review stressed the dearth of research, policy, and practices on the topic of violence and risk management originating from within the field of education (Batsche & Knoff, 1994; Furlong & Morrison; James, 1994; Larson, 1994; Miller, 1994; Morrison, Furlong, & Morrison, 1994; Poland, 1994; Soriano, Soriano, & Jimenez, 1994). Although the recommended method for change differed among the various authors, the need for research on the use of current theory and practices within school-based prevention efforts did not vary (Larson; Morrison, Furlong, & Morrison, 1994). Furthermore, a failure to implement programs that utilize available understandings was even suggested to be unethical, as it would be a disservice to students (Larson).

An effort to provide educational systems practical guidelines for responding to the problem of school violence in our nation's schools was initiated through a collaborative effort between the United States Department of Education and Department of Justice. This collaboration resulted in two reports, with the first being drafted in 1998 and a second in 2000. The first report, entitled *Early Warning, Timely Response: A Guide to Safe Schools* (Dwyer, Osher, & Warger, 1998), provides educational agencies with a reference for understanding risk marks for violence in youth populations as a foundation for school safety planning. The second report, entitled *Safeguarding Our Children: An Action Guide* (Dwyer & Osher, 2000), outlined detailed guidelines for developing and implementing school safety plans based on evidence based practice. The model offered within the report consisted of a three level plan that assists schools in the identification and allocation of services to at risk students.

The first tier of the school safety plan model addresses violence prevention efforts that can be broadly implemented and serve the largest number of students. Interventions at this level might include systemic supports integrated into the general education curriculum or administrative procedures offered on a school based level, e.g., academic remediation, teaching problem solving skills, or using positive discipline. Students who did not respond to this level of intervention would then be identified and provided need specific services based upon their

2

warning signs for violence. Applied Behavioral Assessment is the recommended methodology for identifying students and their specific needs through the use of functional behavioral assessments. The authors suggest that this methodology was recommended due to its familiarity to school professionals. Services provided to these identified students at the second tier might include anger management, individual or family counseling, and the development of a behavioral support plan. The third tier of the model represents service provision at the most intense level that is to be provided to he highest risk students. Students identified at the third tier of the safety plan model represent the highest risk for violence and often require intensive, collaborative, and multifaceted interventions in order to succeed. These interventions may require coordination of community based supports or partnerships with other agencies, e.g., juvenile justice system, to shape services to meet the specific needs of the student and their families (Dwyer & Osher, 2000).

Despite the existence of evidence based practices for assessing violence risk in youth populations, educational professionals have been slow to develop practical applications that utilize available theory and research on violence risk assessment for use in school safety planning (Cornell, 2004; Furlong & Morrison, 2000). Rather, available research suggests that many school officials continue to rely on "zero tolerance" policies to manage situations perceived to be dangerous (Skiba & Peterson, 1999a; Skiba & Peterson, 1999b). Although zero tolerance policies have come under scrutiny for their finality and lack of flexibility or ability to distinguish between degrees of risk posed by students (Martin, 2001; Tebo, 2000), the practical implications suggest that they may even limit school officials' ability to make informed decisions and neglect possibilities for instituting interventions to lessen violence risk (Cornell).

As an alternative to current practices, Furlong and Morrison recommend

What is needed is a thoughtful approach to synthesizing the multidisciplinary knowledge bases that have been created over the past two decades and that: promote the agenda of preventing youth crime, delinquency, and violent behavior while at the same time supporting educators' efforts to create a positive learning environment for all students through specific consideration of relevant school contexts. (p. 75)

In noting the need for professional practices that assist educators to make more informed decisions about violent students, Cornell (2004) suggests that assessment may be a valuable and largely under utilized tool for meeting this need. In light of these recommendations, integration

3

of formalized assessment strategies for identifying and managing violence within our schools may offer a promising solution. Further, by incorporating evidence based practices for violence risk assessment from related fields, assessment may also provide a practical means for synthesizing multidisciplinary knowledge and afford professionals additional resource for guiding intervention.

Violence Risk Assessment

Recent reviews within the field of violence risk assessment suggest that practices over the last twenty years have progressed significantly and offer practitioners promising technological tools, in the form of empirically based methods, for assessing and managing potentially violent individuals (Borum, 1996; Monahan, 1997; Monahan & Steadman, 2001). Although present assessment methodologies benefit greatly from advancements in both conceptualization and understanding of violence risk as a construct, the identification of empirically based risk factors for violent behavior have provided the framework for the development of these current methodologies (Borum, 2000).

The understanding of risk factors for violence specific to adolescent populations has benefited significantly from the empirical attention it has received within the literature (Borum, Bartel, & Forth, 2003). Research efforts in this area have explored a wide variety of topics encompassing aspects related to individual, interpersonal, environmental and developmental differences that manifest over time (Farrington, 1998, 2000; Farrington & Loeber, 2000; Loeber, Farrington, Stouthamer-Loeber, Moffitt, & Caspi, 2001; Hawkins, Herrenkohl, Farrington, Brewer, Catalano, & Harachi, 1998; Hawkins, Herrenkohl, Farrington, Brewer, Catalano, Harachi et al., 2000; Lipsey & Derzon, 1998). The amount and diversity of available information on this subject can be summarized in Lipsey and Derzon's observation that, "The volume of research is sufficiently large to be cumbersome..." (p. 87). With this being said, Lipsey and Derzon's meta-analysis provides a comprehensive means of summarizing the available literature on risk factors, which was based on 34 longitudinal studies and focused on two primary research questions. The first question was to identify what predictor variables or risk factors demonstrate the strongest empirical associations with subsequent violent or serious delinquency. Second, Lipsey and Derzon sought to provide insight into which of the empirical associations had sufficient magnitude to be useful for identifying juveniles at risk for serious or violent

4

delinquency. The nature of these findings was reported using both aggregated effect sizes as well as the weighted means for each categorical risk factor.

In Lipsey and Derzon's (1998) statistical analyses of the data, which grouped participants into either a 6-11 or 12-14 age range based on when the predictor variables were initially assessed, a rank ordering of the strongest predictors of subsequent violence or delinquency at age 15-25 were provided in a comparative fashion. The base rate for violent offending and delinquency in these studies was estimated to have occurred in approximately 8% of the sample ranging in age from 15-25 years. Further, although their summary on the risk factors for both age groups were similar in content, the rank ordering of these factors were notably different. For example, in the 6-11 age range, general offenses (.38), substance use (.30) gender (.26), family social economic status (.24), and antisocial parents were found to be the best predictors of violence. By comparison, in the 12-14 age range, social ties (.39), antisocial peers (.37), general offenses (.26) were found to be the strongest predictors in the first and second rank groupings.

Prior to advancements in the field of violence risk assessment, professionals within the mental health field who were called upon to provide assessments of violence risk utilized decision making practices that were largely clinically based. The methodology used within the various clinically based approaches was typically unstructured and, according to Borum (2000), supported by "clinical and historical information, possibly in combination with some psychological testing such as the MMPI or Rorschach," which was then used to "make inferences about whether a person is dangerous" (p. 1265). Research on the predictive accuracy of the clinical approach was largely unfavorable (Borum; Monahan & Steadman, 2001). Efforts to address issues surrounding predictive accuracy within assessment practices gave rise to two alternative trends within the field. Both trends advocate for the use of a structured assessment methodology that utilizes empirically derived factors for violent behavior in making predictions of future violence risk (Monahan & Steadman).

The first to emerge from the research driven movement within the field were the actuarial methodologies (Borum, 2000). Actuarial approaches to violence risk assessment employ formulas as the preferred method for predicting future violence that rely little on the clinical decision making of the evaluator (Grove & Meehl, 1996). The methodologies of actuarially based approaches are solely reliant on the empirically supported factors that produced a statistically significant relationship to violent behavior in the development of the formulae.

Although debate within the field continues, limitations surrounding the generalizability of actuarially based approaches as well as conceptual changes in the manner in which violence risk is understood gave rise to a second methodology (Borum).

The Structured Professional Judgment (SPJ) model represents a hybrid between the clinical and actuarial models as it relies on both clinically as well as empirically based risk factors in the assessment of violence risk (Borum, 2000). The integration of clinical and actuarial methodologies grew out of desire to incorporate the relative strengths of both approaches as well as minimize their weaknesses (Borum et al., 2003). Although structured, the SPJ model provides a flexible framework that lends itself well to meeting the needs of practitioners in a variety of settings as well as increasing sensitivity to the idiosyncrasies of case-specific information within the decision making process (Douglas & Webster, 1999). Given the benefits of flexibility and sensitivity, Borum and Douglas (2003) suggest, "the SPJ model currently is a 'best practice' approach for comprehensive assessment of violence risk, and may be emerging as a desirable standard of practice" (p. 102).

Violence risk assessment in schools. Currently, professionals are being faced with an ever increasing demand for assessments of violence risk as a means of guiding professional judgment and decision making regarding a variety of behaviors of concern (i.e., generalized violence, threats for targeted violence, and sexual offending) and across a variety of settings (i.e., correctional, judicial, educational) (Borum, 2000). Within the field of education, incidences of mass murders within our nation's schools have contributed significantly to this increased demand on educators (Small & Dressler-Tetrick, 2001; Vossekuil et al., 2002).

In response to the need for violence risk assessment in schools, professionals within the field of education, drawing predominately on research and practices from related fields, have developed best practices models to assist educators to more reliably and accurately identify students who may engage in targeted types of violent behaviors. More importantly, recommended practices in the field of assessment seek to move beyond outdated models that conceptualize violence risk in terms of identification or prediction toward including a focus on intervention, management and treatment for decreasing an individual's level of risk for violence (Borum, 2000, 2003; Fein et al., 2002; Vossekuil et al., 2002). As far as this author is aware, the

6

current integrative trend has not been extended to include protocols for the assessment of generalized violence within the educational setting.

Although evidence based practices for assessing generalized violence currently exist, the development of assessment instruments specifically designed to assist practitioners to assess generalized violence risk posed by youth is in its beginning stages (Borum, 2000). Two assessment protocols have been developed using the Structured Professional Judgment model for use with early childhood and adolescent populations; the *Early Assessment Risk List for Boys* (EARL-20B; Augimeri, Webster, Koegl, & Levene, 1998) and the *Structured Assessment of Violence Risk in Youth* (SAVRY; Bartel, Borum, & Forth, 2000), respectively. Both instruments have been published and are currently being made available for practitioners within a variety of settings.

The current edition of the *Early Assessment Risk List for Boys* is in its second version (EARL-20B, Version 2; Augimeri, Koegl, Webster, Levene, 2001) and has been expanded to provide a specific assessment instrument for girls, entitled the *Early Assessment Risk List for Girls* (EARL-21G, Version 1, consultation edition; Levene, Augimeri, Pepler, Walsh, Webster, & Koegl, 2001). The *Structured Assessment of Violence Risk in Youth* has been revised twice since first being made available to practitioners (SAVRY, Version 1, Borum, Bartel, & Forth, 2002; SAVRY, Version 1.1, Borum, Bartel, & Forth, 2003, Version 1.1). Although efforts to establish empirical support for the validity of the use of the EARL-20B and EARL-21G are ongoing (Augimeri et al., 2001; Koegl, Webster, Michel, & Augimeri, 2000; Levene et al., 2001), the SAVRY has received more attention in the professional literature to date (for a review see Borum et al., 2003). The available empirical studies on the use of the SAVRY have provided support for working with youth populations in juvenile justice (Catchpole & Gretton, 2003; McEachran, 2001) and community mental health settings (Fitch, 2002), but preliminary data on the validity of the SAVRY within the educational setting is notably lacking.

Purpose Statement

Presently, developments in the assessment of violence risk warrants consideration for use within educational settings. In an effort to bridge the current gap between research and professional practices, current assessment approaches have been developed for guiding the estimation of risk level for generalized violence as well as intervention efforts with children and youth who struggle with aggression. Although current assessment approaches reflect sound assessment standards when working with violent children and youth in juvenile justice and mental health settings, research and practice within the field of education has been slow to benefit (Cornell, 2004). In part, mental health practitioners within the field of education may be resistant to utilizing assessment methodologies due to their lack of demonstrated validity within educational settings. To build on the suggestions by Furlong and Morrison (2000), the overlying purpose of this study was to draw on available understandings of violence risk assessment for use within an educational setting. For the purposes of this study, the validity of a structured professional judgment approach for identifying adolescents at risk for generalized violence was applied within an educational setting as a means of addressing questions regarding its generalizability. More specifically, violence risk was estimated using the Structured Assessment of Violence Risk in Youth (SAVRY; Borum, et al., 2003), a validated measure based on the structured professional judgment approach. This study also sought to provide insight into the specific nature or profile of violence risk factors within an educational setting for the purposes of guiding future research efforts.

Delimitations

Although the generalizability of this study is restricted due to sample characteristics, the present study represents a starting point for the use of a decision making model for the assessment of violence risk within educational settings. With this study's goal in mind, youth, ages 12 through 18, enrolled within an alternative educational setting for students with educational disabilities were included in this study. The students at this facility were referred to this educational setting from a single public school district serving nearly 34,000 students who reside in a large metropolitan city in the southwestern part of the United States. Given that the students in this study were enrolled in an alternative educational program, this may represent a defining characteristic of this sample that should be considered when applying these findings to other educational settings.

This study also employed only one approach for the assessment of violence risk by using the Structured Assessment for Violence in Youth (SAVRY; Borum, Bartel, & Forth, 2003), an assessment tool that was developed using the Structured Professional Judgment model (Borum et al., 2003). The decision to use the SAVRY is based on the need for a systematic means to consistently measure violence risk in youth populations. As such, this study does not address all possible risk factors and environmental percipients that may be linked to violence within youth populations; rather, it will address those factors included within the SAVRY in order to provide a systematic means for evaluating the validity of this single approach and the accuracy of this measure for distinguishing between violent and non-violent youth within an educationally based setting.

Significance

The significance of this study is ultimately assessed in its ability to provide mental health practitioners with an evidence based practice for identifying students at risk for violence as well as directing intervention efforts to assist identified youth. Additional benefits of this study relate to the specific information gained regarding the types of factors most strongly associated with violence risk in this population. Further, with specific risk factors identified through the assessment process, psychologists and other practitioners may be better equipped to prevent and manage violence in our schools. This research seeks to provide educators with the necessary tools to make informed decisions regarding the manner in which they deal with potentially violent students on their campuses. Furthermore, the information derived from this research presents opportunities for building upon these understandings in the development educationally based interventions for students at risk for violence.

Educational Implications

The educational implications of this research are to provide mental health professionals functioning within education systems with an established methodology for discriminating between violent and non-violent students. A secondary, but related, benefit of this research study is to reinforce the need to develop interventions that target specific risk factors for students who demonstrate elevated risk for generalized violence. Finally, through an improved understanding of the potential for intervention, educational professionals in policy and decision making roles may utilize information from this study to guide their management strategies for students identified as being at risk for future violence.

Theoretical Orientation

Historically, the study of violence has drawn on a broad range of theoretical orientations in an effort to identify and conceptualize the many multifaceted factors associated with violence (McEachran, 2001). While Douglas, Cox, and Webster (1999) ground the practice of violence risk assessment within a scientist-practitioner framework, many current theories of violent offending in youth seek to integrate knowledge from a variety of orientations such as biology, social learning, behavior analysis, cognition, and development (Elliott, 1994; Farrington, 1998; Hoge & Andrews, 1996; Loeber, Farrington, Stouthamer-Loeber, Moffitt, and Caspi, 2001).

The Farrington Theory (Farrington, 1998) of youth violence provides an established model reflecting the current trend in criminological theorizing. It seeks to increase explanatory power through the integration of existing knowledge about risk factors for violence potential in youth (Farrington & Loeber, 2000). In an effort to integrate both developmental and situational theories, The Farrington Theory suggests that long-term influences on an individual (such as, biological, psychological, family, peer, community, and so forth) contribute to the development of 'between-individual differences' that are conceptualized as being static and form the foundation for an individual's violence potential. However, the probability for violence is conceptualized as a process of interaction with more transient or state dependent 'within-individual differences,' (such as being angry or intoxicated) and situational motivators (such as opportunities or access to potential victims). This interaction between long- and short-term individual differences is mediated by an individual's cognitive processes, which include perceptions of cost to benefit ratios, risk, behavioral repertoires, as well as consequences. Finally, within this theoretical framework, feedback effects on the learning process are also postulated to mediate an individual's long-term violence potential as well as decision making process (Farrington). Taken together, the strength of The Farrington Theory is its ability to capture the complex nature of violence potential as a construct given the variability noted both between individuals as well as across situational and environmental contexts. The relevance of the Farrington Theory to the process of violence risk assessment may be measured by its ability to provide a conceptual framework to guide decision making about information gained through the utilization of valid risk assessment instruments (Farrington & Loeber).

10

Research Questions

1. Does the SAVRY distinguish between violent and non-violent adolescents, as evidenced by Total Scores on the SAVRY, within an educationally based sample?

2. Do the three key risk factors (social ties, general offending, and antisocial peers) identified within Lipsey and Derzon's meta-analysis on adolescents ages 12-14 years discriminate between violent and non-violent adolescents as assessed by the SAVRY factors Peer Rejection, History of Non-violent Offending, and Peer Delinquency in this educationally based sample?

3. Which of the four domain scores measured by the SAVRY (Historical Risk Factors, Social/Contextual Risk Factors, Individual/Clinical Risk Factors, Protective Factors) discriminate between violent and non-violent adolescents?

Definition of Terms

Adolescent: A child who is at least 12 years of age, but not yet 19 years of age.

Antisocial Peers: Based on Lipsey and Derzon's (1998) meta-analysis, a key factor includes affiliations with antisocial peers, peer criminality, and peer normlessness.

General Offenses: A key factor in Lipsey and Derzon's (1998) meta-analysis that was measured as crime (index/serious), crimes (mixed), property crimes, recidivism, or status offenses.

Historical Risk Factors: A domain of the SAVRY that includes factors based on past behavior or experiences and is generally static or not subject to change.

History of Non-Violent Offending: A risk factor in the SAVRY that is defined as "any criminal or delinquent activity that does not involve battery such as theft, burglary, drug sales, and serious property destruction" (Borum et al., 2003, p. 25). Although this item relates to illegal behavior, the scoring of this item is not conditional upon formal charges or convictions having been made.

Individual/Clinical Risk Factors: A domain of the SAVRY whose factors focus on attitudes as well as psychological and behavioral functioning.

Key Risk Factor: Risk factor identified as strongest predictor of violence or serious delinquency in Lipsey and Derzon's (1998) meta-analysis using weighted effect sizes.

Non-violent Adolescent: Any adolescent within the sample who does not commit a single act of violence within the academic school year in which they are enrolled at the assessment site.

Peer Delinquency: Peer delinquency refers to an adolescent's social involvements with peers who are involved in delinquent or criminal activities, including gang membership.

Peer Rejection: Risk factor on the SAVRY that is scored based upon an adolescent's experience with peer rejection. Rejection is differentiated both in its intensity and chronic nature. It is generally defined as "adolescents who are liked by few, if any, peers and who are actively disliked by most" (Borum et al., 2003, p. 54).

Protective Factors: A domain of the SAVRY that address factors that can reduce the negative impact of a risk factor or otherwise act to diminish the probability of a violent outcome.

Risk Factor: "Factors that predict a high probability of violence" (Farrington, & Loeber, 2000, p. 733).

SAVRY: The Structured Assessment of Violence Risk in Youth (SAVRY): Version 1.1 (Borum, Bartel, Forth, 2003).

Social/Contextual Factors: A domain of the SAVRY that considers the influence of interpersonal relationships, connection to social institutions, and the environment.

Social Ties: Includes instances of few social relationships and/or low popularity (Lipsey & Derzon, 1998).

Total Score: Score derived from the summation of the twenty-three items comprising the Historical Risk Factors, Social/Contextual Risk Factors, and Individual/Clinical Risk Factors sections minus the score derived from the six items in the Protective Factors section.

Violence: "An act of battery or physical violence that is sufficiently severe to cause injury to another person or persons (i.e., cuts, bruises, broken bones, death, etc.), regardless of whether injury actually occurs; any act of sexual assault, or a threat made with a weapon in hand" (Borum et al., 2003, p. 23).

Violent Adolescent: Any adolescent within the sample who commits a single act of violence, as defined by the SAVRY, within the academic school year in which they are enrolled at the assessment site.

Chapter 2

Review of the Literature

The present chapter will expand upon the concepts and ideas summarized in the introduction. More specifically, the concept of violence will be address as a foundation for further discussion regarding the relationship of empirically supported risk factors to violence prediction. Turning the focus to assessment, distinctions are drawn between the types of violence risk assessment and methodologies, with a detailed review of their etiology provided. Finally, the present chapter will conclude with a review of violence risk assessment practices within educational settings and provide suggests for modifying these practices through the use of a Structured Professional Judgment model.

As Furlong and Morrison (2000) point out, the definition and usage of the term 'school violence' has varied widely. In citing an overall increase in the use of this term in both popular press and empirical publications in recent years, these authors caution that the term 'school violence,' has historically been poorly defined and used as a 'catchall term.' This vagueness presents serious limitations to the application of empirical methodologies, regardless of the field of practice. Furlong and Morrison conclude their review by suggesting that the term 'school violence' may actually represent a "multifaceted construct that involves both criminal acts and aggression in schools, which inhibit development and learning, as well as harm the school's climate" (p. 72).

Furlong and Morrison's (2000) definition of school violence parallels contemporary conceptualizations within the field of violence risk assessment that view risk as a contextual (based on situations or circumstances), dynamic (susceptible to change), and continuous (varying in degree) construct (Borum, 2000). The multifaceted quality inherent in Borum's definition is also reflected in the current methodologies used to assess violence (Douglas & Ogloff, 2003a). Assessment approaches, such as the Structured Professional Judgment (SPJ) model, emphasize the use of semi-structured assessments based on empirically supported risk factors in order to guide professional judgments regarding violence risk as well as identify areas for intervention (Borum, 2003; Douglas & Kropp, 2002).

In the field of violence risk assessment, risk factors are generally understood to represent indicators, derived from empirical study and professional literature, that have been associated with an increased risk of violent or delinquent offending (Borum, 2000; Farrington & Loeber, 2000). Although contributions to the understanding of the risk factors for violent youth have received significant empirical attention within the literature, the summarization of this information for practical applications can be difficult and cumbersome (Lipsey & Derzon, 1998; Bloomquist & Schnell, 2002). Prior to reviewing specific risk factors for violence, an overview of violence in childhood and adolescent populations is provided.

Violence in Youth Populations

Empirical efforts to understand violent behavior have focused on identifying characteristics that distinguish violent from non-violent individuals (Lipsey & Derzon, 1998). With respect to youth populations, particular emphasis has been placed on contextualizing antisocial behavior within a developmental framework (Farrington, 1998, 2000; Farrington & Loeber, 2000; Loeber et al., 2001; Hawkins et al., 1998; Hawkins et al., 2000). Longitudinal research designs have contributed significantly to the growing body of knowledge in the field of violence risk assessment that has improved understandings of population characteristics, such as prevalence rates, distinctive subtypes and risk factors. Points of convergence within the literature indicate that violent youth are heterogeneous in nature and demonstrate many common characteristics with their non-violently delinquent counterparts (Bloomquist & Schnell, 2002). Thus, violent offenders represent a specific subset within a broader population that is typically categorized in the literature as serious juvenile offenders (Loeber, Farrington, & Waschbusch, 1998). When reviewing this growing body of literature for the purpose of identifying risk factors specific to violence, mental health practitioners are presented with difficulties due, in part, to the methodological issues associated with manner in which offending is defined (Cottle, Lee, and Heilbrun, 2001). While serious juvenile offenders can be further categorized under the taxonomy of general juvenile delinquency, the narrowing of focus to specific, albeit relatively infrequent, characteristics of these subgroups allows for the establishment of diagnostically relevant differences that lend themselves well to prevention and intervention efforts (Bloomquist & Schnell, 2002; Borum, 2003; Hawkins et al., 2000).

Observations made through the study of risk factors over time in youth populations has also given rise to the formulation of developmental models that have identified pathways or typologies within the general juvenile delinquent population. These models suggest that youth who present a higher risk for violence may be distinguishable from non-violent offenders, demonstrate a pattern of behavior that is progressive in nature, and follow a particular developmental trajectory (Farrington & Loeber, 2000; Frick, Barry, & Bodin, 2000; Lober et al., 1998; Loeber et al., 2001). Drawing on longitudinal data generated by the Pittsburgh Youth Study, Loeber et al. (2001) identified three different developmental pathways to delinquency. The stability of these patterns across samples lead Loeber et al. (2001) to suggest that the, "...onset of various levels of delinquency seriousness suggested that individuals' development toward serious forms of delinquency may be orderly" (p. 348). In this model, the identification of specific risk factors coupled with subsequent patterns of behavior is used to differentiate between an "overt pathway," a "covert pathway," and an "authority conflict pathway."

The "overt pathway" starts with minor aggression that progresses to incidences of physical fighting and then to juvenile violence, a pattern characterized by the repetitive use of aggression rather than positive problem solving (Loeber et al., 2001). The "covert pathway" begins with frequent lying and minor shoplifting that later leads to acts of property damage and finally serious non-violent delinquency such as burglary (Farrington & Loeber, 2000). Finally, the "authority conflict pathway" is defined by the onset, prior to age twelve, of stubborn behaviors that progress to defiance and later authority avoidance such as running away (Loeber et al.).

The implications of the pathway model are summarized by Loeber et al. (2001) who suggest that it may represent, "... a way to help identify youth at risk and optimize early interventions before problem behavior becomes more stable and worse over time" (p. 350). Taken a step further, the implications of empirical trends also provide compelling support for the need to establish assessment techniques that can be used to identify these "at risk" youth and align early intervention efforts to risk factors that are specific to the individual as well as environment. With this in mind, a review of the literature on risk factors identified as markers for future violent behavior in youth will be discussed. The emphasis of this review will be placed on understanding how these factors are identified and how they are utilized in the conceptualization of violence risk. Beginning with Lipsey and Derzon's (1998) meta-analysis, longitudinal studies focusing on the developmental etiology of juvenile offending will be used to illustrate contemporary understandings in the area of violence risk assessment.

Risk Factors

As noted previously, risk factors are defined as variables that have been demonstrated empirically to be associated with higher probabilities for violence (Farrington & Loeber, 2000). However, as Lipsey and Derzon (1998) note, "An essential first step in assessing the prospects for using risk variables diagnostically is to assess the nature and predictive strength of those variables that are presumed related to subsequent delinquency" (p. 87). To this end, Lipsey and Derzon attempted to synthesize the longitudinal research using meta-analytic procedures with two goals expressly stated. The first was to identify what predictor variables or risk factors demonstrate the strongest empirical associations with subsequent violent or serious delinquency. Second, their study sought to provide insight into which of the empirical associations had sufficient magnitude to be useful for identifying juveniles at risk for serious or violent delinquency.

The Lipsey and Derzon (1998) meta-analysis was conducted using both published and unpublished research studies that were coded into a database that indexed the strength of association between the predictor variable and criterion variable in terms of effect sizes. Their database also included codes for descriptive information of the studies reviewed, such as methods, procedures, and samples. Statistical analyses allowed for control of between-study differences that could confound comparison and aggregation of the empirical findings in terms of relative strength of the different predictor variables. The inclusion criteria used for gathering the data for these analyses utilized only prospective longitudinal studies of the development of antisocial behavior. Further, restrictive criteria were established for violent behavior and serious delinquency, which were defined as physical aggression or the threat of physical aggression and index offenses or offenses of comparable seriousness. The final sample identified 793 effect sizes based on 66 reports of 34 independent studies.

Although several steps were taken to minimize possible issues associated with dependency within the 793 effect sizes, the final synthesis yielded 155 aggregated effect sizes that were then further subdivided by age ranges in which the predictor variable had been assessed. The data was then summarized by organizing these variables into categories according to the constructs assessed for both a 6-11 and 12-14 age range that was compared to violent or serious delinquent behavior during adolescence and early adulthood. The meta-analysis results yielded 18 and 19 predictor constructs for each age range, respectively, that were rank ordered

18

using weighted hierarchical multiple regression analyses. The rank orderings were divided into five groupings based upon the boundaries of the confidence intervals around the regression adjusted estimates of the aggregated effect sizes. The predictor variables for both age ranges are presented in order from strongest to weakest in Table 1.1. Effect sizes for both age groups ranged from a high of .39 to a low of .04 (Lipsey & Derzon, 1998).

At first glance (from Table 1), it becomes apparent that there are notable differences in the ordering of risk factors across the 6-11 and 12-14 age groupings. In view of these findings, Lipsey and Derzon (1998) conclude "These factors not only have diagnostic value for identification of high-risk juveniles, but they also suggest that disruption of early patterns of antisocial behavior and the peer support for such behavior may be an especially promising strategy for preventive intervention" (p. 101). Applying this to the assessment process, two important concepts are noted. First, the dissimilarity between the two age groups highlights the importance of understanding the influence specific factors have on clinical judgments concerning individual risk ratings. Second, individual risk ratings must be understood within a broader developmental context that takes into consideration the trajectory of antisocial behavioral patterns in youth. The combination of these two understandings is particularly important for the clinician seeking to develop interventions designed to target identified risk factors.

Table 1

Ranked order based on strength of effect size of predictor variables by age groupings. [1]

Age 6-11 Predictors	Age 12-14 Predictors
General offenses	Social ties
Substance abuse	Antisocial peers
Gender (male)	General offenses
Family SES	Aggression
Antisocial parents	School attitude/performance
Aggression	Psychological condition
Ethnicity	Parent-child relations
Psychological condition	Gender (male)
Parent-child relations	Physical violence
Social ties	Antisocial parents
Problem behavior	Person crimes
School attitude/performance	Problem behavior
Medical/physical	IQ
IQ	Broken home
Other family characteristics	Family SES
Broken home	Abusive parents
Abusive parents	Other family characteristics
Antisocial peers	Substance abuse
	Ethnicity

Note: [1]Based on "Predictors of violent or serious delinquency in adolescence and early adulthood," by M.W. Lipsey and J.H. Derzon, *In Serious and Violent Juvenile Offenders: Risk Factors and Successful Interventions*, edited by Rolf Loeber and David P. Farrington (Sage Publications, Inc., 1998).

Seeking to provide linkages between the growing body of empirical literature concerning the development of violent behavior in youth populations and evidence based practices within educational settings, the validity of Lipsey and Derzon's (1998) findings were explored by the present study for applicability within educationally based assessment practices. For the purposes of the present study, parallels are made between Lipsey and Derzon's (1998) results and the risk factors measured by the SAVRY. For the 12-14 age range, Lipsey and Derzon (1998) identified the strongest risk factors as social ties ($r = .39$), antisocial peers ($r = .37$), and general offenses ($r = .26$), which can be measured by the Peer Rejection, Peer Delinquency, and History of Non-Violent Offending on the SAVRY. More specifically, social ties, as measured by the SAVRY risk factor Peer Rejection, is encapsulated in the Peer Rejection factor that is operationalized as "children or adolescents who are liked by few, if any, peers and who are actively disliked by most" (Borum et al., p. 54). Similarly, the risk factor capturing antisocial peer relationships on the SAVRY is the Peer Delinquency factor that is assessed by the adolescents affiliation with "other youth who regularly engage in antisocial acts and/or is involved in gang activities or is a gang member" (Borum et al., p. 53). Finally, general offenses are measured by the SAVRY risk factor History of Non-Violent Offending. The History of Non-Violent Offending factor takes into account the frequency with which an adolescent has engaged in non-violent, antisocial behaviors such as "...stealing, property destruction, smoking, selling drugs, and early intercourse (before 14 years old)..." (Borum et al., p. 25).

Although the Lipsey and Derzon 's (1998) meta-analysis provides insights into possible trends and contributions of specific risk factors to the prediction of youth violence, further discussion concerning the developmental characteristics that differentiate violent youth is warranted. A brief review of two well established longitudinal studies will be examined as a framework for organizing a discussion concerning the clinical judgment process generated through the analysis of individual risk factors and the development of behavioral patterns in youth populations.

The Cambridge Study in Delinquent Development (Farrington, 2000; 2002) and the Pittsburgh Youth Study (Loeber et al., 2001) represent two established research projects that lend themselves well to such a comparative analysis. With this in mind, findings from the two projects will be reviewed for the purpose of illustrating the manner in which risk factors are empirically derived as well as the contributions this research offers to understanding the development of violent behavior over time in youth populations. In the interest of parsimony, this synopsis will be narrowed, when feasible, to those factors suggested to be strong predictors of violence risk in adolescent populations.

The Cambridge Study in Delinquent Development (Farrington, 2000) was a prospective longitudinal survey of 411, predominately white, males who were followed between the ages of 8 and 40 years. After being contacted initially in 1961-1962 through local school registries in London, the main purpose of the study was to measure as many factors as possible that were understood to be causes or correlates of offending and antisocial behavior. Data collection procedures entailed school based assessments at ages 8, 10, and 14 that established baseline. Follow up interviews were then conducted at ages 16, 18, 21, 25, and 32. Retention rates were reported to be high, falling between 95% and 94% at ages 18 and 32, respectively. Information concerning antisocial behavior were assessed through record review searches at the Criminal Record Office for documentation of convictions. These convictions did not include crimes that were considered to be minor, such as common assault, traffic infractions and drunkenness. Although the most common offences were noted to be thefts, burglaries, and "unauthorized taking of vehicles," there were numerous cases of offenses for violence, vandalism, fraud, and drug abuse. In addition to official records, self-reports of offending were also obtained from the participants beginning at age 14 and continuing through age 32.

Although multiple analyses have been conducted using data from the Cambridge study, Farrington (2000) concluded his summary of the analyses of predictors for adolescent violence to date by stating, "The most important childhood predictors of adolescent violence include troublesome and antisocial behavior, daring and hyperactivity, low IQ and attainment, antisocial parents, poor child-rearing (harsh and erratic discipline, poor supervision), parental conflict and broken families, low family income and large family size" (p. 35). More specifically, for the purposes of comparison, a study was conducted investigating the strongest predictors of aggression at age 12-14, self-reported violence at age 16-18, self-reported fights at age 32, and convictions for violence between ages 10 and 32. Using regression analyses, the best predictors of convictions for violence between ages 10 and 32 included high daring (taking many risks), authoritarian parents, a convicted parent, low verbal IQ, and harsh parental discipline (for more information see Farrington, 1989). It is also worthy to note that subsequent analyses of this data have also yielded results to suggest that violent youth tend to be more versatile in their patterns of offending and problem behavior by comparison to non-violent offending peers (Farrington, 2002).

Similar in design to the Cambridge Study in Delinquent Development (Farrington, 2000, 2002), the Pittsburgh Youth Study (Loeber et al., 2001) uses a prospective longitudinal survey design in order to research the development of juvenile offending, mental health problems, and drug use in a sample of inner-city youth. The sample was comprised of three approximately equal groups of males ages 7, 10, and 13 (total $N = 1517$). In establishing the groups, prospective participants were screened to ensure that approximately half of the group consisted of high risk and half average to low risk based on pre-existing risk factors. Further, for the entire sample approximately half were African American and half were White (Loeber et al.). Unlike the Cambridge Study, the Pittsburgh Youth Study was correlational rather than predictive, with the risk factors and problem behaviors being measured in a concurrent fashion (Farrington, 2002).

Follow-up in the Pittsburgh Youth Study was conducted with the participants, their teachers, and parents on half-yearly intervals, which entailed nine assessments for the youngest group, seven assessments for the middle group, and six for the oldest group. Although the middle sample was later integrated into the other two groups when they began to overlap in age, data collection in the beginning stages of this study necessitated the completion of just over 9,000 assessments per year. Similar to the Cambridge study, the purpose of the Pittsburgh Youth Study was to measure constructs purported to be causes or correlates of delinquency. Given the magnitude of information gathered through this process, the researchers refer to the assessments in terms of waves. Future assessments are to be continued on a yearly basis until the youngest group is 20 years of age and the oldest sample reaches age 25.5. Assessments included formal measures, interviews, and review of educational records, such as California Achievement Test scores. The criterion measures for the Pittsburgh Youth Study used official records of offending, gathered through searches in the Juvenile Court of Allegheny County, self-report, as well as parent and teacher reports of delinquent or antisocial behavior. Retention rates in the Pittsburgh Youth Study were also high, for example 92.0% and 89.7% of the participants in the youngest group completed the 12th and 13th waves of data collection, respectively.

Prevalence rates for serious delinquent offenses within the Pittsburgh Youth Study were differentiated by risk grouping, age and race. Serious delinquency was operationally defined as offenses that included car theft, breaking and entering, strong-arming, attack to seriously hurt or kill, forced sex, or selling drugs. Trends within the data demonstrate a general increase in antisocial behaviors over time in the high risk group. However, the nature of this increasing trend was noted to differ in the African American and White participant groups. For example, at age 15, cumulative onset for African American participants reached 51.4% while only 28.1% for white participants. Similarly, prevalence rates at age 16 in these two groups was reported as 26.6% for African Americans and 18.7% for white participants.

Similarly, frequency of serious offending was also noted to follow a trajectory that increased with age. Race differences were again noted with the African American group engaging in more frequent acts than the white group. Review of court records indicated prevalence rates for serious delinquency in the middle and oldest groups were 29.7% and 44.6%, respectively. With respect to violence committed by the sample, the review of court records yielded prevalence rates for index violence of 11.9% and 14.7% for the middle and oldest groups, respectively (Loeber et al., 2001).

Viewing these findings over time, risk factors identified within the Pittsburgh Youth Study were examined within the context of their relationship to the three developmental pathways discussed previously, overt, covert, and authority conflict. Given that the focus of the present study is primarily interested in violence, summarization of the factors associated with the Overt Pathway and violent or aggressive offending, more specifically, will be addressed here. Combining data from both the Cambridge study and Pittsburgh Youth Study (Loeber et al.), these authors reported that the strongest predictors for violence in these two studies were low guilt, low achievement, young mother, broken family, single mother, low SES, family on welfare, and "bad" neighborhood (based upon census data or parent report).

From an assessment perspective, variability within these findings exemplifies the heterogeneous nature of this population. Building on our understandings of risk factors, these findings also illustrate the need for assessment methodologies that incorporate the multifaceted and variable characteristics of factors as they pertain to biological, social, and environmental influences on the individual. However, conceptualization of violence risk must account for the progression of these factors over time. In this sense, historical risk factors become important to formulating educated opinions regarding risk for future violence. Finally, an understanding of the developmental pathway demonstrated by an adolescent provides a barometer for their ability to successfully adapt and master tasks necessary for adjustment within a particular functional domain (Bloomquist & Schnell, 2002). Ideally, the integration of this information within the assessment process through a combination of clinical judgment and empirically based knowledge enables the practitioner to link intervention efforts to the individual needs of each child.

Implications for Intervention

Before concluding the present discussion of risk factors, a brief review of the distinction made within the literature on the nature of risk factors as well as its relevance for assessment and intervention is also warranted. Risk factors can be distinguished based on their amenability to change due to time, situation, or a combination of both. Static risk factors represent those indicators that are either historical or dispositional in nature, while dynamic factors tend to be more heavily represented by individual, situational, or social indicators. As this nomenclature suggests, dynamic factors are also distinguished from static factors in terms of their propensity for change over time and through intervention (Borum, 2003). For the purposes of linking assessment to intervention, differentiations made between static and dynamic risk factors hold importance in terms of case conceptualization and treatment planning (Borum, et al., 2003).

To summarize, violent youth represent a heterogeneous subgroup within the broader juvenile delinquent population. Within the assessment process, it is important to note that risk factors often differ both in nature and relevance based on the population (e.g., adult, adolescent, or early childhood), the context in which they are assessed (e.g., school, community, or inpatient setting), as well as the type of violence being assessed (e.g., generalized verses targeted violence) (Borum, 2000; Douglas, Cox, & Webster, 1999). With the ever increasing body of literature studying the etiology of specific types of violence, categorization of violent acts is an important distinction. For the purposes of the present study, a distinction between targeted and generalized forms of violence will be discussed in more detail.

Targeted Versus Generalized Violence

The terms generalized and targeted violence are used to distinguish between two types of violence that differ in their predictive indicators, prevalence rates, and behavioral manifestation (Reddy, Borum, Berglund, Vossekuil, Fein, & Modzeleski, 2001). Generalized violence, as the term suggests, is broad in nature and encompasses behavioral acts, both reactive and proactive in nature, that represent serious violations of another person's or persons' rights and are severe enough to cause physical harm or even death. Examples of generalized violence within school setting might include physical fights, sexual assault, or use of a weapon to threaten another person (Borum, et al., 2003). By comparison, targeted violence represents a specific form of violence in which both the perpetrator and target or targets are selected prior to the violent act (Borum, Fein, Vossekuil, & Berglund, 1999; Reddy et al., 2001; Vossekuil et al., 2002). Examples of targeted acts of violence within our nation's schools include those incidences of mass murder such as the one at Columbine High School on April 20th, 1999.

The distinction between targeted and generalized violence is important on many levels. First, as noted previously, the prevalence, or base rate for particular types of violence vary and as Reddy et al. (2001) note with regard to generalized violence, "Identifying children and adolescents who are at risk for violent behavior, broadly conceived, is not particularly difficult…violent behavior during adolescence is so common that, in some groups, it is virtually normative" (p. 160). Within a developmental framework, adolescence is frequently when the risk of antisocial behavior is highest (Moffitt, 1993). Second, with increased awareness regarding the etiology and nature of specific forms of violence, research findings suggest that specific methodologies or approaches may be necessary when conducting assessments of risk for specific types of violence as well as with different populations (Borum, 2000; Cornell, 1990; Douglas & Webster, 1999; Reddy et al.; Fein, et al., 2002; Vossekuil, et al., 2002).

Violence Risk Assessment in Schools

Although relatively new by comparison to other fields of study, such as clinical or forensic psychology, the origins of current violence assessment models influencing educational practice today can be traced from two different, but related, trends within the field of violence risk assessment. First, and most recent, is the model that was developed by the *Safe School Initiative*. The recommendations outlined by the *Safe School Initiative* were based largely on their review of the 37 cases of mass murder in schools occurring with the United States since 1974. The goal and underlying premise of the *Safe School Initiative* was to adapt current understandings regarding the procedures for assessing threats of violence developed by the United States Secret Service's National Threat Assessment Center to the problem of targeted acts of violence within schools (Fein et al., 2002).

26

The current assessment procedures employed by the United States Secret Service are grounded predominantly in the work of Robert Fein and Bryan Vossekuil at the National Violence Prevention and Study Center (Vossekuil et al., 2002). Using a retrospective case study methodology, Fein and Vossekuil (1999) reviewed the thinking and behavior patterns of individuals who carried out or attempted lethal attacks on public officials or prominent persons in the United States since 1949. Using the data generated from this study, investigative procedures were developed for use by the United States Secret Service and served as the model for the development of the school based approach focusing on warning signs or indicators for potential violence (Fein et al., 2002).

The second notable influence in the development of assessment practices for violence risk has emerged in response to recommendations from the Departments of Education and Justice in conjunction with the American Institutes for Research. The purpose for this collaborative was to provide schools with assistance in the development and implementation of violence prevention plans (Dwyer & Osher, 2000). These guidelines outline a comprehensive three-level approach to prevention, which can be found in the report *Safeguarding Our Children: An Action Guide* (Dwyer & Osher, 2000). This action guide recommends the use of functional behavioral assessments as a means of identifying the needs of potentially violent students who have come to the attention of school based team due to their evidencing early warning signs for violence. These early warning signs are analogous to risk factors in as much as they were selected by the authors based upon review of empirical literature identifying them as potential precursors to violence (Dwyer, Osher, Warger, 1998). However, the authors clearly point out that these early warning signs are intended as general indicators that a child may need help rather than actually posing a risk for violence. In this respect, these early warning signs are less specific in their relationship to violence than risk factors. A list of these warning signs has been provided in Table 2. However, for readers interested in reviewing these early warning signs in detail, a copy of the report can be obtained from the internet at
http://www.ed.gov/about/offices/list/osers/osep/gtss.html.

From an assessment perspective, the use of early warning signs is somewhat less clear. Given their primary purpose is for identification and referral, the use of warning signs in the form of a checklist is deemed "inappropriate – and potentially harmful" by the authors (Dwyer, Osher, Warger, 1998, p. 8). Rather, educationally based teams are encouraged to use functional behavioral assessment methods for assessing violence potential. This recommendation was based upon the familiarity of this method to school based professionals as well as its suitability for adaptation to a variety of situational needs (Dwyer & Osher, 2000). These authors advocate the use of this assessment process to "identify the contextual factors that contribute to the behavior" and to "predict the circumstance in which the problem behavior is most or least likely to occur" (Dwyer & Osher, p. 24). While a potential strength of this assessment process is its promise for linking need with interventions, the three-level model for school safety plans lacks a formalized methodology for assessing violence risk.

Table 2

Early warning signs for violence [2]

Social withdrawal	Expression of violence in writings or drawings
Low school interest or poor academic performance	Intolerance for difference and prejudicial attitudes
Excessive feelings of isolation or being alone	Uncontrolled anger
Excessive feelings of rejection	Patterns of impulsive and chronic hitting, intimidating, or bullying others
Being a victim of violence	History of discipline problems
Feelings of being picked on or persecuted	Past history of violence and aggressive behavior
Drug use and alcohol use	Affiliation with gangs
Inappropriate access to, possession of, and use of firearms	Serious threats of violence

Note: [2] Based on Dwyer, K., Osher, D., & Warger, C. (1998). *Early Warning, Timely Response: A Guide To Safe Schools*. Washington, D.C.: U.S. Department of Education.

The practices outlined by these methodologies provide direction to school professionals on identifying students potentially at risk for violence as well as developing interventions aimed at reducing risk or modifying behavior. Unfortunately, a systematic means for investigating or attending to all of the factors known to contribute to risk or establishing a particular student's level of need is notably lacking. The absence of such a protocol presents particular barriers to educational based teams attempting to proactively address student need based on factors influencing their risk for violence. In view of this gap, exploring opportunities for integrating evidence based practices that provide a framework for conceptualizing violence risk seems like a reasonable next step toward improving school safety.

History of Violence Risk Assessment

Historically, the central question surrounding violence risk assessment as a field of study has been its validity, which was based primarily on practitioners' predictive accuracy (Borum, 1996, 2000; Douglas & Ogloff, 2003b; Monahan & Steadman, 2001). Early research efforts dating back to the 1970's portrayed a pessimistic view of practitioners' ability to accurately predict violence (Borum, 1996; Monahan, 1996; Monahan & Steadman, 1994; Monahan & Steadman, 2001). More specifically, research reviews of the predicative accuracy of clinical predictions twenty-five years ago, although limited in number and scope, reported 'true-positive rates' of only 20 to 35 percent (Monahan & Steadman, 2001). A review of these early studies concerning the predictive accuracy of violence risk assessment lead Monahan (1981) to conclude that:

> psychiatrists and psychologists are accurate in no more than one out of
> three predictions of violent behavior over a several-year period among
> institutionalized populations that had both committed violence in the past
> (and thus had a high base rate for it) and who were diagnosed as mentally
> ill. (p. 77)

Since Monahan's (1981) seminal work, developments within the field of violence risk assessment, especially with regard to research, methodology, and practice, have changed dramatically and, in turn, the perception of practitioners' ability to assess violence risk accurately and reliably (Douglas & Ogloff, 2003b). More recent reviews of the empirical research that have included these current developments within the field have yielded more optimistic results indicating that mental health professionals have at least a "modest ability" to predict violence that are significantly better than chance (Mossman, 1994, Borum, 1996, 2000).

To elaborate, increased optimism on the part of many researchers has been linked to developments within the field of violence risk assessment that includes improved knowledge regarding the nature of violence as well as methodologies for measuring it (Borum, 1996; Douglas & Webster, 1999; Monahan, 1996; Otto, 2000; Douglas & Ogloff, 2003a). For example, Douglas and Ogloff (2003b) contend that "these advancements have come with greater understandings of risk factors that increase accuracy and validity for the prediction of future violence" (p. 573), while other researchers have focused on the developments in practice and prevention as underlying these more recent advancements (Borum; Monahan & Steadman, 2001). Improvements in present practice of violence risk assessment were summarized in Otto's (1992) literature review in which he concluded "changing conceptions of dangerousness and advances in predictive techniques suggest that, rather than one in three predictions of long-term dangerousness being accurate, at least one in two short-term predictions are accurate" (p. 130).

Current conceptualizations of violence risk assessment. Current violence risk assessment practices can be traced from the historical origins of early work in violence prediction and its changes in conceptualization over time. It is important to understand the changes in the conceptualization of violence prediction in order to provide a framework for how it relates to present practices within the field of assessment (Borum, 2000; Borum, Swartz, & Swanson, 1996). Prior to the work of researchers such as Monahan (1981) who studied the predictive accuracy of violence assessment by mental health professionals, the working model for violence prediction was based largely upon the notion that an individual's dangerousness was based upon a dispositional characteristic that was static and dichotomous (Borum, 1996, 2000). This working model was based heavily on clinical judgment and was largely unstructured in terms of the manner in which these assessments were conducted (Grove & Meehl, 1996).

In an effort to improve the reliability with which professionals assessed violence potential, a focus on empirically derived risk factors emerged within the mental health profession that produced actuarial formulas that were developed as a means of distinguishing between individuals who were more likely to act out violently and those who would not (Borum, 1996; Borum, Otto, & Golding, 1993; Monahan, Steadman, Silver, Appelbaum, Robbins, Mulvey et al., 2001). Although more reliable, debate continues with regard to the use of statistical equations in risk assessment due to limitations regarding generalizability and utility for guiding intervention (Borum & Douglas, 2003; Monahan, 1997). Given the noted limitations, many of these actuarially based assessment instruments may be less advantageous for use within educational settings or for use across different risk assessment tasks (Borum & Douglas; Borum et al., 1999; Reddy et al., 2001).

Empirical emphasis within more recent assessment practices for violence potential has also contributed to changes in the way violence risk is conceptualized. Contemporary models of violence risk assessment suggest that violence is best understood as a contextual, dynamic, and continuous construct (Borum, 2000). Within this conceptual shift, the task of the mental health professional is not to determine whether or not an individual is a "dangerous person," but rather the level of risk an individual may pose for particular types of behaviors within various contexts and given specific conditions (Douglas et al., 1999; Eaves, Douglas, Webster, Ogloff, & Hart, 2000).

Current changes in thinking and practice have given rise to a third model for violence risk assessment termed 'Structured Professional Judgment' (SPJ; Borum et al., 1999; Borum, 2000; Borum et al., 2003). The SPJ model draws on both empirically derived risk factors as well as clinical judgment in order to guide the assessment of an individual's risk for violence. This model represents a broadening of purpose that emphasizes intervention rather than prediction. Although relatively new, the preliminary research has suggested that Structured Professional Judgment models perform better than unstructured clinical assessments and as well as or better than actuarial predictions (Borum, 2003; Borum & Douglas, 2003; Hanson, 1998). In order to fully grasp the integrative nature of the SPJ model, a brief synopsis of its origins in both the actuarial and clinical models will be necessary.

Actuarial verses clinical judgment models. In an effort to further clarify the distinction made between "clinical" and "actuarial" prediction methodologies within the literature, Grove and Meehl (1996) provided definitions that have been applied by others (see Borum, 2000; Monahan, 1996). According to Grove and Meehl, clinical judgment is conceptualized as representing an "informal, 'in the head,' impressionistic, subjective conclusion, reached by a human clinical judge," while actuarial prediction is "a formal method" that "uses an equation, a

31

formula, a graph, or an actuarial table to arrive at a probability or expected value, of some outcome" (p. 294).

A debate within the field of violence risk assessment continues with regard to the use of statistical equations versus decision making models for the purposes of predicting violence risk (Douglas & Ogloff, 2003b). Although statistical formulas have empirical support (Dawes, Faust, & Meehl, 1989; Grove, Zald, Lebow, Snitz, & Nelson, 2000), the use of statistical equations in risk assessment has been cautioned due to limitations regarding the adaptability of these instruments for more general purposes (Borum, 2000), as well as over simplification of the assessment process (Borum, 2003). As such, many of these actuarially based assessment instruments may be limited or unfeasible for many risk assessment tasks (Borum, et al., 2003; Melton, Petrila, Poythress, & Slobogin, 1997; Monahan, 1997). With the noted limitations in mind, Borum (1996) suggests that the function of these actuarial instruments may vary:

> At a minimum, these devices can serve as a checklist for clinicians to
> ensure that essential areas of inquiry are recalled and evaluated. At best,
> they may be able to provide hard actuarial data on the probability of
> violence among people (and environments) with a given set of
> characteristics, circumstances, or both. (p. 948)

The current controversy surrounding the use of actuarial methods gave rise to a second method for assessing violence risk. Drawing on contemporary understandings of violence as a contextual, dynamic, and continuous construct (Borum, 2000, Borum et al., 2003), researchers have proposed using an integrated model that utilizes both actuarial methods, through the use empirically supported risk factors, and clinical methods, using judgments based upon the consideration of case specific variables such as the base rate for a particular population, the salience of factors for the individual, and the relationship of identified factors with situational or contextual variables (Borum, 2000; Borum et al.; Douglas et al., 1999). By conceptualizing violence risk within this multifaceted framework, the assessment process also seeks to identify areas or risk factors that may guide treatment efforts to lessen an individual's risk for violence (Borum, 2003; Borum et al.; Douglas et al.; McEachran, 2001).

The structured professional judgment model. The incorporation of current changes in thinking into practice was the foundation for a decision making model for violence risk assessment which has been referred to within the literature as "structured clinical judgment" (Hart, 1998), "structured professional judgment" (Douglas & Kropp, 2002), and "guided professional judgment" (Borum et al., 1999; Borum, 2000). Although terminology has differed somewhat, the conceptualization of the structured model itself has not. According to Borum, Bartel, and Forth (2003), "The structured professional judgment approach helps to focus the evaluator on relevant data to gather during interviews and record reviews, so that the final judgment, although not statistical, is well informed by the best available research" (p. 4). Taken together, this decision making model represents a hybrid that draws on both empirically derived risk factors as well as clinical judgment in order to guide the assessment of an individual's risk for violence. The preliminary research evaluating the utility of the Structured Professional Judgment (SPJ) model for assessing violence risk has been promising (Borum, 2003; Borum & Douglas, 2003; Douglas, Ogloff, & Hart, 2003; Hanson, 1998).

To date, the Structured Professional Judgment (SPJ) model has been applied in the development of numerous assessment tools differentiated by the population and type of violence assessed. For example, the *Early Assessment Risk List for Boys* is designed to assess violence potential and delinquent tendencies in males under the age of 12 years (Augimeri, Koegl, Webster, and Levene, 2001), while the *Structured Assessment of Violence Risk in Youth* incorporated risk factors related to assessing generalized violence potential in adolescent populations, ranging in age from 12 to 18 years (Borum, Bartel, & Forth, 2003). As Douglas and Webster (1999) note, the *Historical/Clinical/Risk Management-20* (Webster, Douglas, Eaves, & Hart, 1997) serves the same purpose of assessing violence risk in adults, while violence specific assessment tools have also been developed for domestic violence and sexual assault, i.e., the *Spousal Assault Risk Assessment* (Kropp, Hart, Webster, & Eaves, 1999) and *Sexual Violence Risk – 20* (Boer, Hart, Kropp, & Webster, 1997), respectively.

Structured Assessment of Violence Risk in Youth (SAVRY)

The SAVRY was developed to address the need for an instrument designed for the assessment of generalized violence risk in adolescent populations (Borum, 2000). According to Borum et al. (2003), the SAVRY was modeled after the *Historical/Clinical/Risk Management-20* (HRC-20; Webster et al., 1997) in terms of its structure, but modifications were made in the item content to include risk factors derived from research and literature on child development,

33

violence, and aggression specific to adolescence. The instrument is comprised of twenty-four risk factors that are used to make up the three sections labeled Historical, Social/Contextual, and Individual Risk Factors. The SAVRY also includes a Protective Factors section with six items, which represent moderator variables that have been shown to reduce an individual's risk for violence (Borum et al.).

As noted previously, the SAVRY is currently in its third edition since being made available to practitioners in a Consultation Version (Bartel et al., 2000b). Although the basic structure of the SAVRY has remained consistent, the most recent revision changed one of the Individual Risk Factors content items. The Low Empathy/Remorse item was created to replace the Psychopathic Traits item, which was assessed by using *The Hare Psychopathy Checklist – Youth Version* (PCL-YV) (Borum et al., 2003). As outlined by the authors, the rationale for this change was based on three main points. First, the purpose of the SAVRY is to measure "traits as a 'risk marker' for violence" rather than the construct of psychopathy. Second, the user qualifications for the SAVRY and the PCL-YV differ. Lastly, the negative connotations of the term "psychopath" may bias the interpretation of information gained from the use of the SAVRY. The item Low Empathy/Remorse was created in order to account for some of the variables unique to the construct of psychopathy without necessitating such a diagnosis be made in order to score the SAVRY (Borum et al., 2003).

Preliminary research on the psychometric properties of the SAVRY suggest that the reliability and validity support its use for assessing the risk for predicting future violent offending in adolescent populations within juvenile justice and community mental health settings (Borum et al., 2003; Catchpole & Gretton, 2003; Fitch, 2002; McEachran, 2000). The methodologies of these preliminary studies use retrospective analyses to score the SAVRY through a review of records or case files. Outcome measures consisted of longitudinal follow-up using criminal charges and convictions (Catchpole & Gretton), grouping participants based on violence recidividism (McEachran), and using the History of Violence item as the criterion measure (Fitch).

Although the findings of this preliminary research support the use of the SAVRY to assess violence risk in adolescent populations, a need for additional research that can demonstrate its generalizablity to other populations is indicated (USF, 2005). Given that the SAVRY items were derived from a comprehensive review of the current empirical and professional literature on violent and delinquent youth and theoretically grounded on the SPJ approach, the applicability of the SAVRY to adolescents from diverse back grounds and within a variety of different settings is promising.

The present study was based on previous research assessing the predicative validity in juvenile justice settings (Catchpole & Gretton, 2003; McEachran, 2001) and measuring risk factors within specific populations (Fitch, 2002). A detailed review of the previous research using the SAVRY will be provided for the purposes of comparison with the present study. Although all of the previous studies used retrospective file based reviews to code and score the SAVRY, the methodology, analyses, and findings from these studies will also be reviewed with particular emphasis on the portions that pertain to the SAVRY specifically.

In a study of exploring the predictive validity of The Psychopathy Checklist: Youth Version (PCL:YV; Forth, Kosson, & Hare, in press) and the Structured Assessment of Violence Risk in Youth (Bartel, Borum, & Forth, 2000b) for predicting violence recidivism, McEachran (2001) completed both assessments for 108 young offenders, ages 12-17, admitted for a court ordered psychological and psychiatric assessment at the Youth Services Inpatient Assessment Unit in Burnaby, British Columbia. Prior to completing the assessments, the sample was grouped by a research assistant into three groups of equal sizes based on categories of recidivism, which included violent recidivism, non-violent recidivism, and no recidivism. The assessments were completed by the primary investigator through a retrospective file review and outcome data were gathered through researching provincial conviction records for the participants between the ages of 18 and 21. The predictive validity of the two assessment measures was evaluated using a variety of statistical analyses including analyses of variance, correlations, receiver operator characteristics, odds ratios, logistic regression analyses, and survival curve analyses. Interrater reliability was also calculated by having a second coder rate 36 randomly chosen archival files. Using intraclass correlation coefficients (ICC), reliability was calculated for total scores on both measures as well as for the subscales. The SAVRY yielded ICC estimates of .83 for the Total Score, .85 for the Historical subscale, .80 for the Contextual subscale, .82 for the Clinical subscale, and .73 for the Protective subscale. The Clinical Ratings were found to yield an ICC of .72. The ICC for the Total Score on the PCL:YV was .85, with estimates of factor 1 and 2 yielding scores of .81 and .87, respectively.

35

The means and standard deviations were reported for the SAVRY Total Score and each of the four domains by group. For the violent recidivism group, the means were as follows: Total Score = 29.39, Historical domain = 11.11, Social/Contextual domain = 10.69, Individual/Clinical = 8.03, and Protective Factors domain = .44. Among the non-violent recidivists group, mean scores for the scales were reported as Total Score = 27.25, Historical = 10.64, Social/Contextual = 10.67, Individual/Clinical = 6.33, and Protective Factors domain = .39. Finally, within the non-recidivists group, the means were reported as Total Scores = 19.47, Historical = 7.58, Social/Contextual = 8.08, Individual/Clinical = 4.94, and Protective Factors domain = 1.36 (McEachran, 2001).

McEachran's (2001) initial analyses used one-way analyses of variance (ANOVA), with post-hoc comparisons made using Tukey's test for pairwise comparisons of group differences on continuous variables. Categorical data were explored using chi-square analyses, with phi coefficient for pairwise comparison of group means. The results generated from the ANOVA analyses suggested that the mean scores were significantly different for the Total score and all four subscales across all three groups. In view of the pairwise comparisons from the ANOVA analyses, McEachran concluded that "...the SAVRY clinical structured ratings of risk appear to function well as a predictive tool in helping to distinguish between those young offenders who will go on to recidivate violently, non-violently, or not at all in young adulthood" (p. 50). However, the SAVRY scores, with the exception of the Clinical scale, did not do well in distinguishing between the violent and non-violent groups, but rather only those that would recidivate from those who would not (McEachran).

Point-biserial correlations were used to measure the association between the SAVRY and violent outcome, which was used as an estimate of effect size. Given the low base rate for violent re-offending, these analyses were not suggested to provide a good estimate of the effect size for violent recidivism. With this in mind, the correlations on the SAVRY scales and violent recidivism were as follows: Total score (.32), Historical (.25), Contextual (.20), Clinical (.39), Protective (.18), and Rating of risk (.67) (McEachran, 2001).

Receiver Operator Characteristics (ROC) analyses were conducted as a measure of predictive accuracy. The ROC weighs the true positive rate against the false positive rate to plot a curve and the area under the curve (AUC) provides an index of predictive accuracy. The AUC range from 0, a perfect negative classification, to 1.0, a perfect classification of violent offenders as violent, with .5 representing chance predictions. The AUC for the SAVRY scales were as follows: Total score (.70), Historical (.67), Contextual (.63), Clinical (.72), Protective (.39), and Rating of risk (.89) (McEachran, 2001).

Odd ratios (ORs) were also calculated for violent recidivism due to their practical appeal and resistance to distortion due to sample size. More specifically, ORs are calculated with nonparametric tests of the differences between medians (X^2) and tests whether the distribution of ORs differs as a function of group membership. As McEachran (2001) notes, "An OR of 2.50 means simply that one group (here, the group scoring above the median on a particular instrument) is 2.5 times more likely than some other group (here, the group scoring low) to possess some criterion (here, violent recidivism subsequent to turning 18 years of age)" (p. 57). The association between the SAVRY high versus low scores and violent recidivism suggested that adolescents scoring high on the SAVRY were approximately 1.66 times more likely than those scoring below the median to have been convicted of a violent offense subsequent to turning 18 years of age (McEachran).

Logistic regression analyses were used to determine the proportion of variance accounted for by the two instruments, the PCL:YV and the SAVRY, over violent recidivism. However, it is important to note that the logistic regression analyses incorporated both the PCL:YV and SAVRY in the equations, which, therefore, necessitates that both instruments be reported in the findings. Using a backward elimination procedure, two logistic regression analyses were conducted. The first logistic regression analysis compared the explanatory power of the Total and Factor scores on the PCL:YV and the Total and domain scores on the SAVRY with violent recidivism. The final model derived from this analysis suggested that these instruments were a moderate predictor of violent recidivism that correctly classifying 47.20% of violent cases, 88.90% of non-violent cases, and 75.00% of all cases, X^2 $(1, N = 108) = 25.24, p < .001$. The second logistic regression analysis compared the explanatory power of the Total Factor scores on the PCL:YV, the Total and domain scores on the SAVRY, and SAVRY ratings of risk. The final model derived from this analysis suggested that it was a strong predictor of violent recidivism that correctly classified 88.3% of violent cases, 90.3% of non-violent cases, and 88.0% of all cases, X^2 $(1, N = 108) = 61.55, p < .001$ (McEachran, 2001).

The final analyses conducted in McEachran's (2001) study used survival curve analyses in order to account for between-subjects variability in the length of actual follow-up over time.

The Kaplan-Meier method was used to evaluate the predictive validity of high versus low scores. Thus, the survival curve analyses evaluated how quickly participants scoring high versus low recidivated violently subsequent to turning 18 years of age. The results of the survival curve analysis using the SAVRY did not yield significantly different results for adolescents who scored high versus low over time (McEachran, 2001).

The conclusions drawn from McEachran's (2001) study are many fold and beyond the scope of this brief synopsis. However, it is important to note that one of the underlying purposes of this research was to provide a comparative analysis of the two measures studied, such as The PCL:YV and the SAVRY. Therefore, McEachran framed her findings in this light. With this in mind, McEachran (2001) suggests that "the most beneficial use of the SAVRY in the youth justice system may be as a violence risk/needs instrument guiding intervention strategies, treatment placements, and/or program evaluations" (p. 89). Recommendations for future research on the SAVRY were also provided and highlight the need for cross-validation research exploring reliability and validity issues, such as interrater reliability, test-retest reliability, inter-item reliability and construct validity. Of particular note, McEachran suggests that differences in interrater reliability found between the scale scores and clinical ratings of risk may be suggestive of differences in training and experience between raters that may affect the accuracy of rating of risk for violence (McEachran).

More recently, a similar study was conducted by Catchpole and Gretton (2003), which was published in the professional journal *Criminal Justice and Behavior*. Catchpole and Gretton examined violent and non-violent recidivism and the predictive validity of three instruments, the Structured Assessment of Violence Risk in Youth (SAVRY; Borum, Bartel, & Forth, 2002), Psychopathy Checklist: Youth Version (PCL:YV; Forth et al., in press), and the Youth Level of Service/Case Management Inventory (YLS/CMI; Hoge & Andrews, 2002). A sample of 74 participants was obtained from two sites in British Columbia, Canada. The first site was a facility for incarcerated youth from which 33 male youth ages 15 to 19 were participants. The second site was an outpatient psychiatric assessment and treatment facility. A total of 41 youths, consisting of 30 males and 11 females, convicted of violent offenses were selected to be in the final sample. All three of the measures were coded based upon retrospective file review and outcome data on violent re-offenses were gathered after a 12 month follow-up period using criminal charges and convictions obtained from British Columbia Corrections files (Catchpole & Gretton).

Catchpole and Gretton's (2003) data analyses were conducted using Receiver Operator Characteristic (ROC) and survival analyses. The computation of an ROC analyses results in the development of a curve from which the area under the curve (AUC) can be used as a measure of accuracy. The AUCs for the SAVRY in Catchpole and Gretton's study yielded findings of .74 for the total score and .73 without the psychopathy item, which was removed from the scale in later revisions, with general recidivism. AUCs of .73 were reported for the SAVRY total score (.71 without the psychopathy item) and violent recidivism. Survival analyses resulted in log rank tests that suggested a significant difference between SAVRY risk level and general re-offending, with the high risk group being significantly different from both the low and moderate risk groups. Low and moderate risk groups did not differ significantly. Similarly, with regard to violent re-offending, the high risk group differed significantly from both the low and moderate risk groups. Low and moderate risk groups did not demonstrate a significant difference (Catchpole & Gretton).

Catchpole and Gretton (2003) suggest that their findings lend support for the predictive ability of the SAVRY within their sample of adolescent violent offenders. More specifically, Catchpole and Gretton suggest that moderate to strong relationship between the SAVRY total score and both general and violent re-offending, as indicated by the AUC analyses. Further, the survival analyses suggest that the SAVRY could meaningfully distinguish between low and high risk youth (Catchpole & Gretton).

Finally, Fitch (2002) used the SAVRY to conduct a study assessing the presence or absence of risk factors in a sample of 82 Native American adolescents, 47 male and 35 female. The sample consisted of adolescents, ages 12 to 17, who had been admitted to a residential treatment facility in the southwestern United States for at least 30 days during a 12 month period. The SAVRY was coded in a collaborative manner by the primary investigator and primary therapist at the residential facility using information contained within each participant's case file. The criterion measure used in the Fitch study was violence that had already been committed by the participants prior to being admitted to the treatment facility. Participant records were obtained through file review and used the SAVRY History of Violence item to quantify the variable. Thus, the variable was not included in the calculation of the total score or Historical Risk Factors subscale (Fitch).

Bivariate and multiple linear regression analyses were used to investigate the relationships of each of the risk factor domains to the History of Violence item on the SAVRY. The base rate for violence in this sample was reported as follows: 70% of adolescents had committed three or more violent acts, 23% had committed one or two acts of violence, and only 7% had committed no violent acts. The means for the SAVRY Total Score and each of the risk factor domain scales were provided as follows: Total Score = 34.21, Historical = 12.83 (with the History of Violence factor removed), Social/Contextual = 9.23, and Individual/Clinical = 12.15 (Fitch, 2002).

Results of the regression and correlational analyses in the Fitch (2002) study found that all three risk factor categories as well as total scores on the SAVRY were correlated with violence previously committed by participants, with the strongest predictors being Total Scores ($r = .56$), scores on the Social/Contextual Risk Factors ($r = .54$), scores on the Historical Risk Factors ($r = .48$), and scores on the Individual/Clinical Risk Factors ($r = .48$). Multiple linear regression was used to identify the strongest combination of predictors to violence already committed by participants. Fitch's findings suggest that while all combinations of categories of risk factors were statistically significant, the combination of Social/Contextual and Individual/Clinical risk factor groupings was most significant. However, Fitch cautions that these findings are likely impacted by the removal of the History of Violence item, which has been found to be one of the strongest predictors of violence in studies of risk factors (Bartel et al., 2000b). The Protective Factors subscale was found to have a significant inverse relationship to violence already committed by the participants ($r = -.72$), which is consistent with both the theoretical and hypothesized nature of this subscale (Fitch).

Fitch (2002) also made distinctions between gender differences noted within her findings. More specifically, female participants scored higher on both risk factors as well as protective factors by comparison to their male counterparts. This gender difference was also noted in terms of higher correlations for females than males in all factor groups on the criterion variable, but females were reported to be lower in violence committed (Female $M = 1.49$, Male $M = 1.72$). Drawing on her findings, Fitch suggests that these results point to the importance of the

40

Protective Factors subscale in predictions of violence in adolescent populations, which may also have specific implications based on gender.

In conclusion, preliminary research is encouraging for the use of the SAVRY for predicting youth violence within juvenile justice and community mental health settings. Further, available research has introduced the notion that the SAVRY may be particularly useful for targeting specific areas for intervention to lessen violence risk. Building on the previous research establishing the validity of the SAVRY with select populations, the present study was designed to explore the utility of this methodology for use within an educationally based sample.

Chapter 3

Methodology

This chapter reviews the methodology and design of the present study. A retrospective file review was used to gather data on adolescents ranging in age from 12 to 18 years of age enrolled in a specialized educational facility for emotionally disabled students. The research design of the present study was developed based on a review of available literature researching the validity of the Structured Assessment of Youth Violence (SAVRY) with adolescents in juvenile justice and community mental health settings.

The purpose of the present study is to address current needs within the educational field for a validated assessment method for classifying generalized violence potential as well as identifying areas for possible intervention for students demonstrating elevated levels of risk. In an effort to meet this need, this study utilized the Structured Assessment of Youth Violence (SAVRY) as a measure of violence potential within a sample of adolescents in order to explore its ability to accurately discriminate between violent and non-violent adolescents as well as build on the existing body of knowledge regarding those risk factors that contribute most significantly to elevated risk in this sample of adolescents.

Participants

The accessible population from which this study's sample was drawn included all students between the ages of 12 and 18 years enrolled between the 2003 and 2005 academic school year in a specialized school established to meet the needs of students with emotional disabilities and behavioral challenges located in a large urban school district in the Southwestern United States. The treatment milieu of this facility utilizes a highly structured, behaviorally based token economy system that seeks to teach pro-social skills using a nationally recognized model that has been empirically supported for use with youth who demonstrate significant behavioral and emotional challenges.

The focus of the present study was on adolescents with generalized violence potential. As such, a purposeful sampling methodology was chosen due to its utility for the population and detailed investigation of the selected cases (Gall et al., 2003). The homogeneous nature of the final sample was also beneficial for the purposes of this study because of the higher prevalence rates for externalizing types of behaviors, such as violence, delinquency, academic difficulties,

42

and poor social adjustment, which were characteristics that frequently contributed to these students' placement in the specialized school.

The sample size necessary to achieve the intended purpose of this study was estimated to be 80 cases based on previous research as well as requirements for statistical analyses using Receiver Operator Characteristic (ROC) and Logistic Regression (Leech, Barrett, & Morgan, 2005; Swets, 1996; Tabachnick & Fidell, 2007). Previous research on the SAVRY have utilized sample sizes ranging between 74 and 108 (i.e., Catchpole & Greton, 2003; Fitch, 2002; McEachran, 2001) that yielded significant results. Additionally, Leech, Barrett, and Morgan recommend that a minimum of 20 cases per variable is necessary to achieve adequate power. Thus, with all four SAVRY domains included in the regression analysis, a minimum of 80 cases was deemed necessary.

The working sample for this study was derived from a group of 99 adolescents, ages 12-18, enrolled within the alternative education program during either the 2003-2004, 2004-2005, or 2005-2006 school year. Inclusion in the final sample necessitated that the adolescent had participated in the program for a minimum of four months. Although the nature of this program was designed to be short term based upon the student's individual progress, students who met the inclusion criteria for multiple years within this three year period were included in only their most recent academic year in order to ensure that they are only used once in the final sample. Adolescents for whom there was insufficient information to score the SAVRY were excluded from the sample.

The 99 initial cases reviewed yielded a final working sample of 87 participants. Of the twelve cases excluded from the sample, nine cases failed to meet the four month participation criterion and three cases lacked sufficient information due to incomplete records. For the final sample, missing values within the data set fell within the parameters established within the scoring protocol (i.e., no cases had five or more missing data points). There were 10 cases with missing values, as indicated by an "X" on the scoring protocol, however, none exceeding more than one missing data point. Of these missing data points, no more than three missing values occurred on the same risk factor.

Of the final 87 participants included in the working sample, 82% were male ($N = 71$) and 18% were female ($N = 16$), with a mean age of 14.99 and a standard deviation of 1.65. The ethnic breakdown in the sample consisted of 71% Caucasian, 15% Hispanic, 8% African

American, 2% Native American, and 3% Other. The base rate for committing a violent act, as defined within this study, was observed within approximately 36% of the sample. The vast majority ($N = 82$) of participants' primary area of educational disability was identified as Emotionally Disabled, with approximately 14% of the sample having a secondary eligibility categorization of Specific Learning Disability (see Table 3).

Table 3

Frequency and Percent of Primary, Secondary, and Tertiary Educational Disabilities within the Sample.

Eligibility Category	Primary		Secondary		Tertiary	
	N	%	N	%	N	%
Autism	1	1.10				
Other Health Impairment	1	1.10				
Emotional Disability	82	94.30	3	3.40		
Learning Disability	3	3.10	12	13.80	1	1.10
Mental Retardation			2	2.30		
Speech Language Impairment			4	4.60	3	3.40
None			66	75.90	83	95.40
Total	87	100	87	100	87	100

Psychological and psychiatric reports were also reviewed for diagnostic coding of Axis I disorders as defined by the Diagnostic Statistical Manual of Mental Disorders-Fourth Edition, Text Revised (American Psychiatric Association, 2000). With no formal diagnosis available for 25% of the sample, Attention Deficit/Hyperactivity Disorders and Bipolar Disorders were most heavily represented ($N = 27$, 31%) in this sample (see Table 4). Further, the prevalence rate of comorbid disorders occurred in approximately 37% of the cases reviewed.

44

Table 4

Frequency and Percent of Primary and Secondary Axis I Diagnoses in Sample.

Axis I Disorders	Primary		Secondary	
	N	%	N	%
Attention Deficit Hyperactivity Disorder	27	31.00	7	8.00
Bipolar Disorder	14	16.10		
Oppositional Defiant Disorder	3	3.40		
Conduct Disorder	1	1.10		
Mood Disorder	4	4.60	4	4.60
Post Traumatic Stress Disorder	1	1.10	2	2.30
Intermittent Explosive Disorder	1	1.10	2	2.30
Dysthymic Disorder	2	2.30	1	1.10
Reactive Attachment Disorder	2	2.30		
Depressive Disorder, NOS	2	2.30	1	1.10
Anxiety Disorder, NOS	1	1.10	3	3.40

Related services provided within this alternative educational setting included behavioral intervention (88.50%), nursing (97.70%), counseling (34.50%), speech therapy (11.50%), and occupational therapy (4.60%). Estimates of program attendance were assessed through records of truancies and absences for the academic year. Approximately 20% of the participants in the sample had five or more truancies, with 5% having greater than twenty truancies for the academic year. Absenteeism was also prevalent in this sample with 30% of the sample missing between 10 and 40 days of school. Grade retention was not common, occurring in only 8% of the cases reviewed.

Data was also gathered relative to family composition and background. Only 27% of the participants included in this study were being raised in dual parent homes. Half of the participants, approximately 50%, were being raised within single parent households, with the remaining 22% of the sample being raised by grandparents, in foster homes, in group homes, or by relatives. Approximately 87% of the sample reported English as the primary language used within the home, 12% reported Spanish as the primary language used in the home, and 1% of the sample did not identify a primary language in the home. As an indicator of socioeconomic status, information on participation in the free or reduced lunch program was obtained. Of the cases included in the working sample, approximately 67% of the sample received free or reduced fee lunches.

Violent and Non-violent Offending

As noted previously, violence, as defined by the SAVRY (Borum et al., 2003), includes an act of battery or physical violence that is sufficiently severe to cause injury to another person or persons (i.e., cuts, bruises, broken bones, death, etc.), regardless of whether injury actually occurs; any act of sexual assault; or a threat made with a weapon in hand. (p. 23)

Approximately 36% of the adolescents within the sample committed at least one violent act during the academic year. However, of the 31 individuals observed to be violent, 18 (21%) of the adolescents demonstrated only one violent act, with the remaining 13 (15%) adolescents committing between two and five violent acts.

Rates of non-violent offending were also observed within this sample. Non-violent offending was again defined according the criteria outlined within the SAVRY (Borum et al., 2003), which includes

any criminal or delinquent activity that does not involve battery such as theft, burglary, drug sales, and serious property destruction. Although this item relates to illegal behavior, the scoring of this item is not conditional upon formal charges or convictions having been made. (p. 25)

Of the 87 individuals included within this sample, only 22 (25%) adolescents committed a non-violent offense. Further, of these adolescents, 16 (18%) cases included only one non-violent act while the remaining 6 (7%) cases committed between two and four non-violent acts.

46

Instrumentation (Structured Assessment of Violence Risk in Youth, SAVRY)

The development of the Structured Assessment of Violence Risk in Youth (SAVRY; Borum et al., 2003) was based on the Structured Professional Judgment model and the inclusion criteria for each of the variables contained within this measure was based upon "existing research and professional literature on adolescent development and on violence and aggression in youth" (p. 6). The SAVRY is comprised of 24 risk variables that make up three sub-domains (Historical Risk Factors, Social/Contextual Risk Factors, and Individual Risk Factors) and six protective factors that form a fourth, Protective Factors sub-domain. The traditional protocol for scoring the SAVRY items based upon the detailed coding information contained in the manual uses ratings of high, moderate, or low to score the risk factors. Protective factors are simply scored as either present or absent. However, for research applications, the manual suggests using ratings of "2," "1," or "0" for the risk items and a "1" or "0" for the protective items. Using the numeric coding system, the sum of the 24 risk factor items minus the sum of the six protective factors was used as a theoretically consistent method for deriving the Total Score for the SAVRY. However, for comparative purposes, Total Score calculations based on the 24 risk factor items are also included. Given that the SAVRY was not designed to be a formal test or scale, there are no predetermined cut off scores for interpretation of the Total Score. However, higher scores are generally equated with higher levels of violence risk.

The SAVRY is to be used "to assist professional evaluators in assessing, and making judgments about, a juvenile's risk for violence" (Borum et al., 2003, p. 6). Further, taking into consideration the developmental differences between youth and adult populations, Borum et al., point out that the emphasis on dynamic risk factors within this instrument makes it particularly well suited for use with an adolescent population. The SAVRY may be used to assess either male or female adolescents' ages 12 through 18 years. Although it is important to note that the existing research in this area has been conducted largely with males, available information currently suggests that many risk and protective factors function in similar fashions for both males and females (Borum, 2003; Fitch, 2002).

As noted previously, the SAVRY was not developed to be a formal test or scale. Rather, as Borum et al. (2003) state, "In our view, the primary value of this instrument is to assist in structuring the assessment so that important factors that are well-supported by research will not be missed, and indeed, will be emphasized in formulating a final professional judgment about risk" (p. 13). Given the emphasis on dynamic risk variables, the SAVRY can also be used to guide treatment planning and intervention efforts to reduce violence risk as well as monitor ongoing progress (Borum, 2003; Borum et al.).

Reliability of the SAVRY. The SAVRY manual reports internal consistency analyses of .82 for offenders and .84 for community samples in a study completed during the development and validation of the instrument (Borum et al., 2003). In a study by Catchpole and Gretton (2003), interrater reliability was analyzed using an intraclass correlation coefficient (ICC) that yielded findings of .81 for the SAVRY Total Score and .77 for the Summary Risk Rating. Similar findings were also noted in a study by McEachran (2001), who reported an intraclass correlation coefficient for the SAVRY Total Score and Summary Risk Rating of .83 and .72, respectively.

Validity of the SAVRY. Previous research has demonstrated concurrent, criterion, and incremental validity for the use of the SAVRY. In a published study by Catchpole and Gretton (2003), concurrent validity was examined between the SAVRY Risk Judgment rating and *Youth Level of Service/Case Management Inventory* (YLS/CLI) Summary Classification, reporting correlations of .64, while correlations with the *Hare Psychopath Checklist: Youth Version* (PCL:YV) Total Score were reported to be .68. Comparably, the authors cite findings from their unpublished validation study that found significant correlations with both the YLS/CLI and PCL:YV of .89 and .78, respectively (USF, 2005).

As suggested previously, research on the criterion validity of the SAVRY has consistently demonstrated significant correlations between various outcome measures of violence in juvenile justice and community mental health settings (Fitch, 2002; Catchpole & Gretton, 2003; McEachran, 2001). The publishers of the SAVRY, in reference to an unpublished validation study by the authors (USF, 2005), report significant correlations (rs) between Total Risk Scores on the SAVRY and behavioral measures of institutional aggression (.40) and aggressive conduct disorder symptoms (.52). By comparison, protective factors were found to be negatively related to both outcome measures. These criterion validity findings have been replicated in published research as well. In a study by Catchpole and Gretton (2003), SAVRY

Risk Total Scores were found to correlate significantly with measures of violence in a sample of young male offenders in Canada, (.32), while Fitch found somewhat stronger findings in a sample of high-risk Native American youth (.56). Summary Risk Ratings on the SAVRY have also been found to correlate with violence as an outcome variable. In a study by McEachran, Summary Risk Ratings were also noted to be correlated significantly with violent behavior (.67).

The incremental criterion validity, or predictive power, of the SAVRY has also been demonstrated empirically. Using Receiver Operator Characteristic (ROC) analysis as a measure of predictive accuracy, area under the curve (AUC) for Total Scores have been reported to range between .74 and .80, with .50 equating to predictive accuracy at only change levels (USF, 2005). Moreover, McEachran (2001), using a ROC analysis, reported AUC for SAVRY Total Scores of .70 for predicting violent recidivism within a juvenile justice population. However, when using the Summary Risk Rating the AUC was found to be .89 (McEachran). In the study by Catchpole and Gretton (2003), Summary Risk Ratings were reported to relate to violence recidivism, in that, Low Risk had a 6% recidivism rate, Moderate Risk had a 14% recidivism rate, and High Risk had a 40% recidivism rate. Taken together, these findings lend support for the use of the SAVRY as a structured tool for guiding clinical judgment rather than an actuarial instrument (USF).

Scoring the SAVRY. Item ratings were recorded on a modified version of the SAVRY Coding Sheet (Bartel, Borum, & Forth, 2000a), following established protocols using the numerical rating of "0," "1," or "2" and "X" for items with insufficient information to score. Total scores on the SAVRY were obtained by summing the subscale scores from the Historical Risk Factors, Social/Contextual Risk Factors, and Individual Risk Factors, and then subtracting the subscale scores from the Protective Factors. This scoring method is noted to be theoretically consistent with the Protective Factors being conceptualized as contra-indicators for violence. However, for comparative purposes, Total Scores were also calculated base on the 24 Risk Factors exclusively. According to the guidelines for scoring the SAVRY (Borum et al., 2003), in the event that insufficient information was available to score a factor, an "X" was entered for that item on the coding sheet. Those coding sheets with five or more "X" items were eliminated from the final analyses and the participants were not included in the final sample. The version of the

Coding Sheet used within the present study is included in the Appendix. SAVRY domain and corresponding risk factors are provided in Table 5.

Procedures

After review and approval by both the Local Education Agency and the Institutional Review Board at Northern Arizona University, data were collected during the final month of the school year, May 2006. Given the retrospective nature of the research design, all data collection was completed based on a review of available records maintained by the school district. All sources of information are archival in nature and drawn from the students' special education, psycho-educational, cumulative, disciplinary, intervention, and arrest history contained in their files that were housed as physical records within a secure location at the school. The data collection procedures occurred in two phases.

The first phase of data collection began by reviewing the cumulative files for all prospective students enrolled in all 5th through 12th grade classrooms in the alternative school. This initial file review resulted in the identification of 99 prospective cases, which yielded the final working sample of 87 adolescents.

For the sample's 87 participants, the SAVRY Coding Sheet (see Appendix A) and the Demographic Coding Form (see Appendix B) were completed using the available information contained within the participants' cumulative, special education, and psycho-educational files (see appendix C). Although preferable to base SAVRY scores on interviews combined with file reviews, especially when attempting to score dynamic risk factors, previous studies using this measure have indicated adequate validity using file review alone (Fitch, 2002; McEachran, 2001). The SAVRY was scored by the primary investigator, a Nationally Certified School Psychologist (NCSP) with six years of experience in violence risk assessment and who was professionally trained on the use of the instrument. The SAVRY was scored in accordance with the criteria outlined within the SAVRY manual (Borum et al., 2003).

Additionally, two research assistants, who were also Nationally Certified School Psychologists (NCSP) and professionally trained in the use of the SAVRY, scored approximately 1/3 of the cases selected at random for inter-rater reliability. Random selection of the cases was completed by dividing the sample into two, approximately equal, sets from which a random sample was drawn using a random numbers table.

50

Table 5

SAVRY Domains and Corresponding Risk Factors

Domain	Factors
Historical	History of Violence
	History of Non-Violent Offending
	Early Initiation of Violence
	Past Supervision/Intervention Failures
	History of Self-Harm or Suicide Attempts
	Exposure to Violence in the Home
	Childhood History of Maltreatment
	Parental/Caregiver Criminality
	Early Caregiver Disruption
	Poor School Achievement
Social/Contextual	Peer Delinquency
	Peer Rejection
	Stress and Poor Coping
	Poor Parental Management
	Lack of Personal/Social Support
	Community Disorganization
Individual	Negative Attitudes
	Risk Taking/Impulsivity
	Substance Use Difficulties
	Anger Management Problems
	Low Empathy/Remorse
	Attention Deficit/Hyperactivity Difficulties
	Poor Compliance
	Low Interest/Commitment to School
Protective	Prosocial Involvement
	Strong Social Support
	Strong Attachments and Bonds
	Positive Attitude Towards Intervention and Authority
	Strong Commitment to School
	Resilient Personality Traits

Intraclass correlation coefficients (ICC). Interrater reliability was calculated for the coding of a random sample of the SAVRY assessments using intraclass correlation coefficients (ICC). In remaining consistent with previous research in this area, intraclass correlation coefficients represent a conservative approach to measuring interrater reliability in that they are calculated using relative rank and absolute values (Bartko, 1976; McGraw & Wong, 1996). All 87 cases were scored by the author, a doctoral candidate in counseling psychology and a Nationally Certified School Psychologist (NCSP) professionally trained in the use of the SAVRY (Borum, et al., 2003) with 6 years of experience in violence risk assessment. Two raters were used to code approximately 1/3 of the cases ($n = 25$) selected at random from either the first or second half of the data set. These raters are also Nationally Certified School Psychologists (NCSP) who were professionally trained in the use of the SAVRY (Borum et al.), with Rater 1 having two years experience in violence risk assessment and Rater 2 having five years experience in violence risk assessment. ICCs were calculated for each rater using a one-way random effect model as the index of reliability, while a combined index was also calculated using a two-way random effects model with a consistency definition (McGraw & Wong, 1996). One-way random effects model yielded ICCs of .64 for Rater 1 ($n = 13$) and .90 ($n = 12$) for Rater 2. The two-way random effects model taking into consideration both raters yielded an ICC of .81. Although variation is noted between raters, these reliability coefficients are consistent with previous findings (Catchpole & Gretton, 2003; McEachran, 2001) and are considered acceptable (Bartko; McGraw & Wong).

During the second data collection phase, the outcome measure (see appendix D) was completed by the primary investigator using information collected from the participants' disciplinary, intervention, and arrest history that were routinely maintained in files for each student enrolled within the school. The outcome measure was defined as any act of generalized violence committed during the one year period in which the participant met inclusion criteria for this study. Violence has been defined by the SAVRY (Borum et al., 2003) as

> an act of battery or physical violence that is sufficiently severe to cause injury to another person or persons (i.e., cuts, bruises, broken bones, death, etc.), regardless of whether injury actually occurs; any forcible act of sexual assault; or a threat made with a weapon in hand. (p. 15)

In addition to identifying adolescents who met the criteria for violence, information on the frequency, nature, and date of each incident that meets the definition for violence was collected. Any incident of the non-violent offending recorded during the same academic year was also recorded in similar fashion. Non-violent offending was defined in accordance with the scoring criteria outlined within the SAVRY (Borum et al., 2003) as

> Any criminal or delinquent activity that does not involve battery such as theft, burglary, drug sales, and serious destruction of property...regardless of whether it resulted in formal criminal charge or conviction. (p. 17)

Design and Analysis

The present study employed a correlational design to explore the relationships between the predictor variables measured by the Structured Assessment of Violence Risk in Youth (SAVRY) and the outcome variable outlined within the present study. Multivariate correlations according to Gall, Gall, and Borg (2003) are defined as "any statistical analyses (e.g., multiple regression or factor analysis) that express the relationship among three or more variables" (p. 629). The SAVRY was used in this study to gather aggregate data on the violence potential of participants selected to represent a population of adolescents, ranging in age between 12 and 18 years of age, receiving instruction within a single educational setting. The methodology employed in this study is ex-post-facto, as all data collection was completed retrospectively using available information maintained in the students' physical records (Gall et al.).

For the first research question, Receiver Operator Characteristic (ROC) analyses were conducted. According to Douglas and Webster (1999), the use of the ROC analysis represents recommended practice for determining accuracy because it is influenced less by base rates of a given behavior and it facilitates comparisons of accuracies of prediction under various definitions of "high-risk." ROC analyses are meant to be used with data that have a continuous predictor variable (e.g., Total Score on the SAVRY) and a dichotomous criterion measure (e.g., violent or non-violent). By plotting the true positive proportion of the predictor variable as a function of the false positive proportion, the sensitivity and specificity of the predictor variable can be expressed in the form of a curve, which provides a representation of the overall accuracy of the predictor (Swets, 1996). According to Swets, "The current favored index of accuracy is the proportion of the area of the unit square that lies beneath the ROC, varying from 0.5 at chance performance to 1.0 at perfect performance" (p. 126). Douglas and Webster provided the following interpretation for the resulting area under the curve (AUC) index stating, "A given area represents the probability that a randomly chosen person who scores positive on the dependent measure (i.e., is actually violent) will fall above any given cut-off on the predictor measure, and that an actually non-violent person will score below the cut-off" (p. 190). Using the AUC as an index, an AUC of 0 would represent a perfect negative classification of violent offenders as non-offenders, while an AUC of .5 would be predictive performance at a chance level, and an AUC of 1.0 would be perfect classification of violent offenders as violent (Douglas & Webster; McEachran, 2001; Swets; Swets, Dawes, & Monahan, 2000).

It is also important to note that, because the ROC analysis computes accuracy based upon the sensitivity and specificity of the diagnostic measure, another function of an ROC analysis is to examine decision criteria, which are discussed in terms of threshold or cutoff scores of a particular diagnostic instrument, e.g., the SAVRY. Given that a particular cutoff score or threshold for decision making is not recommended by the authors of the SAVRY (Borum et al., 2003) for theoretical and practical reasons, a variable criterion model will be used when conducting the ROC. Furthermore, although the ROC analysis provides insight into the optimal cutoff scores for SAVRY Total Scores in this population, the cutoff scores will not be reviewed in the results section as it would be counter to recommended practices outlined by the authors.

The remaining two research questions investigate the relationship between the three risk factors identified *a priori* (Peer Rejection, History of Non-violent Offending, and Peer Delinquency) in Research Question 2 and the four domains on the SAVRY (Historical, Social/Contextual, Individual, and Protective Factors) in Research Question 3 with violent offending in this sample. Binary logistic regression is useful when predicting a dichotomous criterion (dependent) variable from a set of predictor (independent) variables that can be continuous, discrete, dichotomous or mixed. By utilizing a logistic regression analysis, a regression equation can be produced that provides an index of the probability of belonging to a particular group based upon a specific combination of predictor variables (Tabachnick & Fidell, 2007).

For the second research question, a binary logistic regression analysis was conducted to determine which of the three risk factors (i.e., Peer Rejection, History of Non-violent Offending, and Peer Delinquency) best discriminate between violent and non-violent adolescents in an

54

educationally based sample. Participants with scores on each individual variable were utilized for the logistic regression analysis. For Research Question 3 a binary logistic regression analysis was conducted to determine which of the four domains (i.e., Historical Risk Factors, Social/Contextual Risk Factors, Individual Risk Factors, and Protective Factors) measured by the SAVRY best discriminate between violent and non-violent adolescents in an educationally based sample. The discriminate validity of the SAVRY was also assessed in this analysis based upon the adequacy of model, with all four domains considered, to correctly classify participants as either violent or non-violent.

Chapter 4

Results

This chapter presents the results from the analyses used in this study. It is organized by research question and the analyses used to address each question. Multiple statistical analyses were conducted each of the three research questions posed within this study. The present study was comprised of a select sample of adolescent students enrolled within a specific alternative educational setting in a large urban school district during the course of three school years, and as such, should be considered when interpreting these results.

Data Screening

Adherence to the prescribed protocol for data screening regarding assumptions prior to analyses (e.g., missing data points, normality, outliers, and multicollinearity), and statistical procedures were conducted using the criteria and guidelines established by Leech, Barrett, and Morgan (2005), Swets (1996), and Tabachnick and Fidell (2007). The screening for skewness and kurtosis by subscale and Total Score did not depart from normality and no potential outliers were present. Tolerance statistics did not suggest concerns with multicollinearity. Based on the working sample of 87, Cronbach's Alpha were computed for each of the four subscales, with a low of .61 noted for the Protective Factors domain and a high of .80 for the Individual Risk Factors domain. The Historical Risk Factors and Social/Contextual Risk Factors domains yielded alpha's of .77 and .73, respectively.

SAVRY Total and Subscale Scores

Descriptive statistics were computed for the SAVRY Total Score with Protective Factors, SAVRY Total Score without Protective Factors, and each of the four domain scales. Of the 87 cases for which the SAVRY was completed, Total Scores with Protective Factors ranged from a low of 0 to a high of 39 out of a possible 48. The mean for Total Scores with Protective Factors in this educationally bases sample was 18.47 with a standard deviation of 9.53. Total Scores without Protective Factors ranged from a low of 3 to a high of 39, with a mean of 20.14 and a standard deviation of 8.53. Out of the possible 20 points on the Historical Risk factor domain, the mean was 6.86 with a standard deviation of 4.00. For the Social/Contextual Risk Factors domain, the mean was 4.71 out a possible 12 points with a standard deviation of 2.40. On the Individual/Clinical Risk Factors domain, the mean was 8.67 out of the possible 16 points with a standard deviation of 3.45. Finally, out of a possible 6 points, the mean for the Protective Factors domain was 1.59 with a standard deviation of 1.25.

Research Question 1

1.   Does the SAVRY distinguish between violent and non-violent adolescents, as evidenced by Total Scores on the SAVRY, within an educationally based sample?

Receiver Operator Characteristic (ROC) analyses were conducted to investigate the ability of the SAVRY to differentiate between violent and non-violent adolescents within the present sample. For comparative purposes, ROCs were also conducted for each of the four sub-domains (Historical, Social/Contextual, Individual/Clinical, Protective) as well as for SAVRY Total Scores calculated with and without Protective Factors.

With regard to the SAVRY Total Score, comparisons between scoring the measure with and without corrections being made for the presence of Protective Factors were investigated. A paired samples t-test comparing the two scoring methods was significant (t (86) = -11.28, $p <$ .001). ROC analyses were used to produce Area Under the Curves (AUC) for both SAVRY Total Scores and each of the domain scales. AUCs, levels of significance, standard errors, and confidence intervals are provided for each of the analyses in Table 6.

The SAVRY Total Score with and without correction for Protective Factors yielded an AUC of .72 and a confidence interval of .61 to .83. This finding is statistically significant ($p =$ .001) indicating that the use of the SAVRY Total Score to correctly identify violent youth outperforms those based on chance predictions alone. The ROC curve for the SAVRY Total Score with Protective Factors can be seen in Figure 1.

Table 6

Areas Under Curves (AUCs) of Receiver Operating Characteristic Analyses for the SAVRY Domain Scores and Total Score

SAVRY	AUC	P	SE	95% CI
Historical	.61	.067	.06	.50 - .74
Social/Contextual	.69	.004	.06	.57 - .81
Individual/Clinical	.75	.000	.05	.64 - .85
Protective	.35	.017	.06	.23 - .46
Total Score with PF	.72	.001	.06	.61 - .83
Total Score without PF	.72	.001	.06	.61 - .83

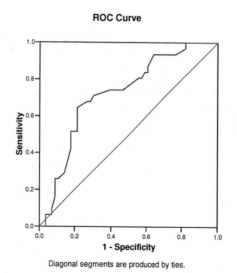

Diagonal segments are produced by ties.

Figure 1. The Receiver Operator Characteristic analysis and Area Under the Curve for SAVRY Total Score with Protective Factors

For comparative purposes, ROC analyses were also conducted for each domain of the SAVRY. With the exception of the Protective Factors domain that yielded an AUC of .35, these findings suggest moderate to strong relationships ranging from a high of .75 for the Individual/Clinical Risk Factor domain to a low of .61 for the Historical Risk Factor domain, with a .69 noted for the Social/Contextual Risk Factor domain. It is important to note, however, that the finding for the Protective Factors domain of .35 is consistent with the theoretical and practical role outlined within the SAVRY. More specifically, the protective factors are conceptualized to represent contra-indicators for violence, which are consistent with present findings.

Research Question 2

2.   Do the three key risk factors (social ties, general offending, and antisocial peers) identified within Lipsey and Derzon's (1998) meta-analysis on adolescents ages 12-14 years discriminate between violent and non-violent adolescents as assessed by the SAVRY factors Peer Rejection, History of Non-violent Offending, and Peer Delinquency in this educationally based sample?

A binary logistic regression was conducted to investigate whether the three identified risk factors (Peer Rejection, History of Non-violent Offending, and Peer Delinquency) discriminate between violent and non-violent adolescents within the educationally based sample. The three predictor variables maintained a minimum suggested sample size of 60 cases for the analysis (Leech, Barrett, & Morgan, 2005).

The SAVRY factors Peer Rejection, History of Non-violent Offending, and Peer Delinquency were selected based on support within the literature identifying these variables as the strongest predictors of violence in adolescent youth. Logistic regression was conducted to assess whether the three predictor variables, Peer Rejection, History of Non-violent Offending, and Peer Delinquency, significantly predicted whether or not an adolescent acted out violently. When all three predictor variables are considered together, they significantly predict whether or not a student was violent, $X^2 = 10.61$, $df = 3$, $N = 87$, $p = .014$. Table 7 presents the odds ratios, which provide an estimate of the odds for estimating correctly who will be violent based on each of the three factors. When considered individually, only History of Non-violent Offending and

59

Peer Delinquency demonstrated a statistically significant relationship to violence ($ps < .05$). The odds ratios within the omnibus equation, however, indicate that the odds of discriminating correctly who will act out violently improve by 57% when information regarding History of Non-violent Offending and 78% when Peer Rejection is known. Further, if one has knowledge of Peer Delinquency the odds of correctly differentiating between violent and non-violent adolescents improves by 133%.

Table 7

Logistic Regression Predicting Who Will Be Violent Based on Empirically Supported Variables General Offending, Antisocial Peers, and Social Ties Measured By the SAVRY

Variable	B	SE	Odds ratio	p
History of Non-violent Offending	.45	.32	1.57	.154
Peer Delinquency	.85	.52	2.33	.104
Peer Rejection	.58	.37	1.78	.116

Research Question 3

3. Which of the 4 domain scores measured by the SAVRY (Historical Risk Factors, Social/Contextual Risk Factors, Individual/Clinical Risk Factors, Protective Factors) discriminate between violent and non-violent adolescents?

A binary logistic regression was conducted to investigate the relative contribution each of domain scores plays in predicting violent and non-violent adolescents. Therefore, logistic regression was conducted to assess whether the four predictor variables, Historical Risk Factors, Social/Contextual Risk Factors, Individual/Clinical Risk Factors, and Protective Factors, significantly predicted whether or not an adolescent committed a violent act. When all four predictor variables are considered together, they significantly predict whether or not an adolescent committed a violent act, $X^2 = 19.24$, $df = 4$, $N = 87$, $p = .001$. Within the present sample, this regression equation correctly classified 82% of those adolescents who were not violent and 45% of those adolescents who were violent. When considered individually, all of the domains demonstrated a significant relationship to violence ($ps < .05$), with the exception of the Historical risk factor domain ($p = .07$). Table 8 presents the odds ratios, which suggest that the odds of estimating correctly who will act out violently improve by 29% if one knows the Individual/Clinical Risk Factors and by 31% when the Social/Contextual Risk Factors are known.

Table 8

Logistic Regression Predicting Who Will Be Violent Based on Domain Scales

Domain Scale	B	SE	Odds ratio	p
Historical	-.14	.10	.87	.161
Social/Contextual	.27	.18	1.31	.128
Individual/Clinical	.25	.10	1.29	.009
Protective	-.13	.28	.88	.640

Summary of Findings

Significant results were found for all three Research Questions. Research Question 1 shows significant predictive validity of the SAVRY Total Score for distinguishing between violent and non-violent youth at significantly better than chance levels. Although a significant difference was noted when the Protective Factors were included in the calculation of the Total Score, the predictive validity did not differ. These results parallel previous research findings within samples of adolescents from juvenile justice and community mental health settings. The practical implications of weighting risk factors based upon previous empirical findings for the purposes of guiding interpretation was explored in Research Question 2 by targeting the strongest predictors of violence noted within Lipsey and Derzon's (1998) meta-analysis, as measured by the risk factors Peer Rejection, History of Non-violent Offending, and Peer Delinquency on the SAVRY. The results within the present study indicate that, while the significance of these factors taken in isolation varies, the predictive significance of these factors is most clearly demonstrated when viewed collectively. Finally, significant predictive relationships were also explored in Research Question 3 for each of the domain scales on the

SAVRY. With the exception of the Historical Risk Factors Domain, all domains scales demonstrated a significant relationship with violence in this educational sample. Implications of this study's findings are discussed in more detail within the following chapter.

Chapter 5

Discussion

In the face of ongoing tragedies within our nation's schools due to violence, a review of
the literature suggests that policy and practice within the field of education may benefit from
methodologies and understandings for violence risk assessment developed within related fields.
Recent advances have given rise to new instruments for the assessment of violence risk. The
focus of the present study sought to build upon the current knowledge base relative to recent
conceptualizations of violence risk and the specific factors that improve identification as well as
treatment for individuals deemed a "high risk" for perpetrating violent acts. To this end, violence
risk assessment methodologies in psychology were reviewed for applicability and utility within
an educational setting.

A structured professional judgment (SPJ) model was selected as a "best practice"
approach due to its integrative origins grounded in both clinical practice and empirical actuarial
modeling that, due to its flexibility, demonstrates promise for generalizability for use within an
educational setting. After review of the available instruments designated for this purpose, the
Structured Assessment for Violence Risk in Youth (SAVRY) was chosen as an established
assessment instrument that has been validated for use with adolescent populations in both
juvenile justice and community mental health settings (Borum, 2000). Previous research has
suggested that the SAVRY is particularly well suited for the identification of potential areas for
intervention to reduce violence risk (McEachran, 2001). Thus, the research questions designed
for this study address the predictive validity of the SAVRY within educational settings as well as
exploring possible differences unique to utilization of this measure with an educationally based
sample. The results of the present study were intended to present mental health professionals
working within the field of education with information concerning potential alternatives for
identifying and managing students who present a high risk for violence. This chapter discusses
the results from the present study, which will be organized by the research question and
relationship to previous research. Practical implications of these findings are noted, as well as
limitations, considerations, and areas for future research.

Differences in Total Scores for Violent and Non-violent Youth

The first research question investigated the predictive accuracy of the SAVRY in discriminating between violent and non-violent adolescents within an educationally based sample. Further, the present study assessed the implications of including the Protective Factors in the calculation of the Total Score in accordance with their hypothesized role of reducing an individual's violence risk. Although inclusion of the Protective Factors significantly lowered the SAVRY Total Score in this sample, this difference did not translate into any changes in predictive accuracy. The present findings continue to underscore the need for further research to clarify the relationship between risk and protective factors as well as their contribution to violence risk. Using the SAVRY Total Score, the results of this study indicate that the SAVRY was able to effectively distinguish between violent and non-violent adolescents within this educationally based sample at significantly better than chance levels. This finding is consistent with previous studies predicting violence recidivism in juvenile justice settings using the SAVRY (Catchpole & Gretton, 2003; McEachran, 2001). However, the present findings are noted to be slightly higher, but well within reported confidence intervals. Thus, the present study's Area Under the Curve (AUC) of .72 likely does not represent an actual difference by comparison to those reported by Catchpole and Gretton (AUC of .71) or McEachran (AUC of .70). These findings add to the growing body of evidence supporting the use of the SAVRY as well as the Structured Professional Judgment model for differentiating between violent and non-violent youth.

Comparisons made between the present study and previous research must take into consideration potential differences in the population characteristics from which the research samples were drawn. Catchpole and Gretton (2003) and McEachran (2001) utilized samples of incarcerated youth within their studies who likely, as a condition of their group membership, possess specific characteristics that may have muted the discriminative power of particular risk factors that contribute to the SAVRY Total Score (e.g., History of Violence, History of Non-violent Offending, or Peer Delinquency). According to McEachran, the juvenile justice population, from which both samples were drawn, represents a homogenous group of adolescents who were referred for psychological or psychiatric assessment and are likely to be Caucasian, to be referred to the courts at a younger age, to have a number of current criminal offenses, and to be charged with a crime against a person. By comparison, the present study's educationally based sample was referred for assessments because of educational and mental health needs rather than criminal behaviors. Although not mutually exclusive, the sample used in the present study likely reflect higher proportions of risk factors unique to the educational setting from which they were drawn, which might include factors such as Poor School Achievement or Low Interest/Commitment to School. These considerations are not limited to empirical comparisons, but also hold relevance for understanding potential relationships of these findings for adolescents within the general population.

Taken together, the present findings contribute to the growing body of literature supporting the use of a Structured Professional Judgment model and, more specifically, the SAVRY as a valuable instrument for assessing violence risk in youth. With the significant findings of the present study, the efficacy of the method and instrument has been expanded for use within educational settings. Although cross validation of the SAVRY does demonstrate some variability in its predictive accuracy, these differences are minimal and may be more reflective of the instruments sensitivity to differences within the populations sampled. More central to the purpose of this study, however, these findings are promising in their support for the use of the SAVRY within educational settings as a means of discriminating between violent and non-violent youth.

Risk Factor Differences for Violent and Non-violent Youth

The second research question explored the relevance and generalizability of longitudinal research that has identified specific risk factors (e.g., Peer Rejection, History of Non-violent Offending and Peer Delinquency) as having greater predicative strength for discriminating between violent and non-violent youth (Lipsey & Derzon, 1998). These results indicate that, when all three factors are considered together, they significantly predicted whether an adolescent would be violent or not. More specifically, the regression equation, with all three risk factors taken together, correctly classified 88% of those adolescents who were not violent and 38% of those adolescents who were violent. However, when considered individually, only History of Non-violent Offending and Peer Delinquency demonstrated a statistically significant relationship to violence. Though not individually significant in conjunction, the odds of correctly discriminating between violent and non-violent adolescents in this sample improved by 57%

when History of Non-violent Offending was known, by 78% when Peer Rejection was known, and by 133% when Peer Delinquency was known.

The findings from Research Question 2 are in general agreement with Lipsey and Derzon's (1998) findings in as much as each of the risk factors improved the odds of correctly discriminating between a violent and a non-violent adolescent within this sample. However, only History of Non-violent Offending and Peer Delinquency demonstrated a statistically significant relationship to violence when considered in isolation. The contradictory aspects indicated by the failure to find a significant relationship between Peer Rejection and violence may be attributable to multiple influences. First, the nature of the social ties variable within Lipsey and Derzon's (1998) study does not constitute an exact equivalent to the Peer Rejection factor on the SAVRY, which, although related, likely does not fully encompass all facets of social ties. Second, the retrospective design used to collect information on these factors limits the potential richness gained from direct measures of behavior, which are central to the assessment of dynamic factors such as Peer Rejection (Borum et al., 2003; McEachran, 2001). Lastly, the possibility of potential correlations between variables having a masking effect within these findings cannot be ruled out.

In summary, although illustrating the importance of utilizing empirically based risk factors for the assessment of violence within educationally based populations, these findings also lend credence to the notion that predictive power is gained when multiple risk factors are used in conjunction, a finding consistent with both McEachran (2001) and Fitch (2002). Conceptually, this notion represents a central tenet of the Structured Professional Judgment approach which seeks to assist evaluators in gathering all relevant data in order to make a well informed judgment (Borum et al., 2003).

These findings also lend themselves to the growing body of literature investigating contributory factors for violence among adolescents within our nation's schools. When the relative contribution of these risk factors are considered, these results are encouraging in view of the potential benefits of preventative efforts targeting specific risk factors that may be amenable to change through the assessment process, i.e., Peer Rejection or Peer Delinquency, in order to reduce an adolescent's violence potential (Borum, 2003).

Domain Score Differences for Violent and Non-violent Youth

In view of the ongoing discussion within the violence risk assessment literature regarding the relative contribution of each of the SAVRY domains for predicting violence (Fitch, 2002; McEachran, 2001), the third research question explored the relationships of the domain scores to violence in this sample. The present findings share both commonalities and dissimilarities with previous research findings.

Results from this study indicate that, when all four domains are considered together, the regression equation correctly classified 82% of those adolescents who were not violent and 45% of those adolescents who were violent, which represents prediction at significantly better than chance levels. Although the underlying factors contributing to this finding are beyond the scope of this study, possible explanations may reflect the error variance associated with this study's methodology, which is notably similar to other study's methodologies investigating the use of the SAVRY. More specifically, the utilization of file review as the sole source of information for coding the SAVRY may have magnified the tendency to underestimate risk factor ratings. Similarly, the measurement of the outcome variable (e.g., violence) was also limited to information gained from reviewing files maintained by the educational agency, which likely underestimates the actual rate of violence committed by adolescents in this sample. Finally, given the implications associated with making a Type II error, these findings may indicate a tendency toward making a Type I error as an alternative to incorrectly identifying potentially violent students. Regardless of the contributing factors, however, the present findings should be considered when interpreting SAVRY results.

When the relative contributions of each domain were assessed within the omnibus model, only the Individual/Clinical domain continued to demonstrate a significant relationship with violence. This finding is consistent with those of McEachran (2001) who also reported stronger associations with violence recidivism for the Individual/Clinical domain and SAVRY Total Score by comparison to their Historical, Protective, and Social/Contextual counterparts. Interestingly, although the present study used only the SAVRY, the predictive strength of the resulting regression equation is noted to be similar to McEachran's, which included both the SAVRY and Psychopathy Checklist: Youth Version (PCL:YV; Forth, Kosson, & Hare, 2003).

Fitch (2002) found positive linear relationships between the SAVRY Total Score and each of three risk factor domains and violence already committed by a sample of Native

American youth in a residential treatment facility. Among the three risk factor domains, however, the strongest correlate with violence was the Social/Contextual domain. Fitch also reported an inverse relationship between the Protective Factors domain and violence, which was stronger than any of the positive relationships among the risk factor domains. Although consistent with both the theory and construction of the SAVRY, the present study's findings provide an illustration of the complex relationship between risk and protective factors on violence risk as well as highlighting the need for ongoing research into understanding the function of contra-indicators for the reduction of violence risk (Fitch).

When the four SAVRY domains were assessed in isolation, these results indicate that only three of the domains demonstrate a significant relationship with violence. The non-significant findings for the Historical Risk Factor domain are puzzling in view of the literature that finds history factors to be among the strongest predictors of future violence (Borum et al., 2003; Farrington, 1991; Mossman, 1994; Parker & Asher, 1987). Comparisons made between previous studies suggest differences in base rates for violence may contribute to this observation. For example, within Fitch's (2002) sample of Native American youth, 93% of the participants had a history of violence by comparison to only 66% of the present sample. Further, out of the maximum possible points allotted to the Historical Risk Factors domain, participants in Fitch's study scored over 71% by comparison to participants in McEachran's (2001) study who scored 56% and 34% in the present study. The present findings are believed to highlight the heterogeneity that is characteristic of disruptive youth as well as the unique contribution rapid developmental change has on this population. This observation has led other researchers to suggest that historical factors may not be as robust a predictor in youth populations as they are in adult populations (Harris, Rice & Quinsey, 1993; McEachran).

Practical Implications

Educational professionals have long recognized the need for efforts to address violence within our nation's schools (Furlong & Morrison, 1994). A barrier to the development of meaningful interventions has been due, in part, to the inherent difficulties distinguishing students who present with a high risk for violence from those who do not (Fein et al., 2002). With the relatively low base rate for violence noted within school settings (DeVoe et al., 2003), violence risk assessment presents a viable method for improving accuracy in identification and guiding intervention (Borum, 2003). Further, these evidenced based practices for assessing violence risk are particularly promising in view of their potential to augment current recommended practices for developing and implementing school based safety plans. Drawing on over 50 years of research, mental health professionals have developed assessment methodologies that reliably and accurately discriminate between potentially violent individuals (Monahan, 1996).

The present study's findings are encouraging with respect to the use of the Structured Professional Judgment model and, more specifically, the Structured Assessment of Violence Risk in Youth (SAVRY) for assessing violence in educational settings. With SAVRY Total Scores correctly identifying 45% of violent and 82% of non-violent youth within the present sample, this instrument offers practitioners a viable means for discriminating between violent and non-violent youth. Furthermore, contextualizing the present findings within the existing research on the SAVRY to date, the sensitivity of the SAVRY to idiosyncrasies within samples is particularly encouraging in view of potential benefits associated with guiding intervention efforts to reduce violence risk (Borum, 2003; McEachran, 2001).

With this in mind, the possibility of sample specific differences reflecting unique differences between populations or settings would seem to discourage professional practices that assign greater relevance to particular factors based upon understandings gained from empirical findings. A dynamic, non-linear relationship reflecting the rapid developmental course of adolescence would seem to provide a better conceptual fit to the variability observed in the pattern of risk factors in relationship to violence within the literature currently. This trend in the literature presents inherent challenges to researchers and clinicians alike who seek to generalize findings that attribute relative importance to specific risk factors. A concordance between the present findings and preliminarily research on the SAVRY better supports practice that utilizes risk factors taken in conjunction to make decisions. Moreover, the present study's findings demonstrate a remarkable amount of consistency in this instruments performance across settings and samples (Catchpole & Gretton, 2003; Fitch, 2002; McEachran, 2001). This is encouraging in view of efforts to develop evidenced based practice in the field of education. Building on these findings, there continues to be a significant need for additional research to guide clinicians in the use of the instrument with different populations and settings. This notion will be elaborated upon later in the section on future research.

Implications for training are also indicated by these results. In view of the variability noted between estimates of interrater reliability in this study, the present findings raise interesting questions regarding the level of training and competency needed to effectively utilize the SAVRY. Within the context of this study, the two raters, both Nationally Certified School Psychologists professionally trained in the use of the SAVRY, differed only in their years of experience completing violence risk assessments. With a difference of only three years, interrater reliability was observed to improve from a correlation of .64 to .90. Although not conclusive, these findings do provide compelling evidence to suggest a need for specialized training and supervision in violence risk assessment. As has been suggested elsewhere (McEachran, 2001), training programs that incorporate the available research reflecting current understandings of risk factors that are predictive of violence as well as the practice in which they are used to guide decision making may provide the best foundation for developing competency in this area.

Limitations and Considerations

Various limitations are characteristic to the nature of research presented in this study. The first potential limitation relates to the homogeneous nature of the sample chosen for this study. While a well established precedence exists for employing retrospective analyses, archival data on participates were limited to adolescents living within an urban environment who were enrolled within a specialized alternative education setting for students with specific learning needs. Limitations attributable to homogeneity are also evident in the proportion of the sample from similar ethnic backgrounds, with approximately 71% being comprised of individuals of European-American descent. Therefore, consideration should be given to these characteristics when seeking to apply these findings to dissimilar populations.

An additional point of caution relates to the use of archival records maintained by the educational institution as a sole source of information. Archival studies have been noted by researchers to be vulnerable to potential bias due to proceduralized record keeping practices as well as missing or limited data (Cornell, 1990; McEachran, 2001). This limitation presents particular difficulties when coding dynamic risk factors, such as Peer Rejection and Peer Delinquency, due to their reliance on contextual or situational information. In view of the present study, this source of potential bias may have introduced a confounding influence on the results that serves to distort the relationship of risk factors to violence in the present sample. However, we must rely on the professional integrity of the record keepers to report and maintain accurate records.

Similarly, violence was also coded using archival information maintained within educational files. Although these records reflected information gathered from multiple sources, such as parent report, police report, and teacher report, this information provides only an approximate estimate of violent acts within this sample. In this regard, the current findings may represent an underestimate of violent behavior, which may have subsequently influenced the present findings.

Future Research

Ongoing research efforts exploring the psychometric properties (i.e., reliability and validity) continue to represent a need for the development of the SAVRY as an efficacious instrument. Future research must continue to establish the test-retest reliability, inter-item reliability, construct validity, and concurrent validity of this instrument across different populations and settings. With this in mind, future research could focus on replication of this study using more heterogeneous educationally based samples in order to provide parameters for the generalizability of the present findings. Furthermore, exploring the utility of the SAVRY for discriminating between violent and non-violent adolescents within traditional educational settings that typically have much lower base rates for violence is also warranted. This line of research would be likely be fruitful for building on the notions that the SAVRY may not only offer insights into identifying youth at risk for violence, but also those dimensions or risk factors that may distinguish these two groups. In this regard, the present findings raise interesting questions regarding qualitative dimensions that may distinguish between adolescents correctly identified by the SAVRY from those adolescents who were not.

Additionally, future research should consider examining the predictive validity of the SAVRY using prospective designs. The use of prospective designs would provide more accurate information regarding the influence of dynamic risk factors on the prediction of violence within adolescent populations. In this respect, future studies would incorporate both file review as well as collateral interviews with students, teachers, and parents. The importance of this line of research is particularly noteworthy for understanding the relative contribution of dynamic factors, such as those contained within the Social/Contextual domain, in conceptualizing violence risk in a developmental context critical to the assessment of adolescents.

Research addressing potential influences of training and experience also represents an area for future empirical attention. Although good interrater reliability was demonstrated by the primary investigator and an experienced research assistant, moderate but acceptable levels of interrater reliability were observed between the primary investigator and a research assistant with less experience in violence risk assessment. In addition to adding to the body of research investigating the psychometric properties of the instrument, this research would also provide insight into potential sources for inconsistency as well as factors that influence variability between raters. Ultimately, this information could be used to develop training programs as well as guiding current practitioners in the appropriate use of the SAVRY.

Finally, research exploring the efficacy of treatments for reducing violence risk in adolescents who present with specific factors identified through the assessment process is needed to establish the direct benefit to students. This line of research would also provide insight into the potential utility of the SAVRY for use within educational settings as means of re-assessing risk over time. In view of the dynamic and contextual nature of the SAVRY, available findings suggest that the SAVRY may be particularly well suited to this task (McEachran, 2001). Moreover, with research suggesting that treatment efficacy increases when guided by assessment (Borum, 2003), the SAVRY presents possibilities for identifying specific areas amenable to change as well as the relative contribution dynamic factors hold for a student's overall level of violence risk. Therefore, research methodologies employing pre-post test designs using the SAVRY may present unique opportunities for outcome research on the changeability of the underlying processes that contribute to violence risk.

Conclusions

The present findings suggest that mental health professionals tasked with the responsibility for addressing ever increasing demands for prevention and intervention programs to decrease violence within our nation's schools may utilize violence risk assessment as a means of discriminating between students who present with a high and low risk for generalized violence. In view of the advancements made within the field of violence risk assessment over the past 30 years, professionals within the field of education stand to gain considerable benefit in their efforts to assist identified students by integrating knowledge and practices from related fields.

The benefits of these practices may be realized, in part, through the integration of validated instruments developed for the assessment of violence risk with adolescent populations into the broader context of school safety plans. Utilization of these assessment tools provides practitioners with a methodology for adhering to professional guidelines reflecting best practice. With emphasis on establishing evidence based practices, assessment approaches offer a means for improving the reliably and validity of information used to guide program development, decision making and treatment planning concerning violence in our schools.

The results of this study provide encouraging evidence for the use of the Structured Assessment of Violence Risk in Youth (SAVRY; Borum et al., 2003) with educationally based populations. The development of the SAVRY, rooted in the Structured Professional Judgment model, represents a promising approach for the identification of adolescents who present a high risk for violence as well as the risk factors that place them at greater risk. By incorporating both static and dynamic factors, the SAVRY also demonstrates promise for the development of effective school violence prevention programs by providing an established practice for identify and intervening with students. These interventions might include guiding disciplinary practices, treatment planning, as well as monitoring violence risk over time.

With a link between treatment efficacy and assessment being suggested elsewhere (Borum, 2003), utilization of the SAVRY within schools may also hold implications for improving treatment programs for identified students through opportunities for program development and evaluation. With the increased demand for using evidenced based practices in schools, the SAVRY may warrant consideration as an instrument for measuring treatment outcomes. Likewise, by limiting ineffective or unnecessary treatment, the SAVRY may also prove useful in guiding the allocation of services.

Finally, with questions raised by this study's findings regarding the level of competency necessary to utilize this instrument effectively, ongoing research efforts will be required in order to fully define the parameters for its use. While the SAVRY is still in many respects in its infancy, continued empirical attention to this instrument and its use within educational settings is supported by the present findings. Future research may seek to build upon the present findings by replicating this study with different educational populations. With this being said, however, the ultimate benefit of this instrument will be assessed in its ability to assist students and the educational professionals who serve them. Optimistically, through more accurate identification, appropriate actions can be taken to reduce violence. Then the data and public perception could reflect the reduced concern of violence within our nation's schools.

References

American Psychiatric Association (2000). *Diagnostic and statistical manual of mental disorders.* Fourth Edition, text revision. Washington, DC: American Psychiatric Association.

Augimeri, L. K., Koegl, C. J., Webster, C.D., & Levene, K. S. (2001). *Early Assessment Risk List for Boys: EARL-20B, Version 2.* Toronto: Earlscourt Child and Family Center.

Batsche, G. M., & Knoff, H. W. (1994). Bullies and their victims: Understanding a pervasive problem in the schools. *School Psychology Review, 23,* 165-174.

Bartel, P., Borum, R., & Forth, A. (2000a). Coding Form. *Structured Assessment of Violence Risk in Youth (SAVRY).* Version 1.1. Author.

Bartel, P., Borum, R., & Forth, A. (2000b). *Structured Assessment of Violence Risk in Youth (SAVRY): Consultation Edition.* Author.

Bartko, J. (1976). On various intraclass correlation reliability coefficients. *Psychology Bulletin, 83,* 762-765.

Bloomquist, M. L., and Schnell, S. V. (2002). *Helping Children with Aggression and Conduct Problems: Best Practices for Intervention.* New York: The Guilford Press.

Boer, D. P., Hart, S. D., Kropp, P. R., & Webster, C. D. (1998). *Manual for the Sexual Violence Risk – 20: Professional guidelines for assessing risk of sexual violence.* Vancouver: British Columbia Institute Against Family Violence.

Borum, R. (1996). Improving the clinical practice of violence risk assessment: Technology, guidelines, and training. *American Psychologist, 51,* 945-956.

Borum, R. (2000). Assessing violence risk among youth. *Journal of Clinical Psychology, 56,* 1263-1287.

Borum, R. (2003). Managing at-risk juvenile offenders in the community. *Journal of Contemporary Criminal Justice, 19,* 114-137.

Borum, R., Bartel, P., & Forth, A. (2003). *Manual for the Structured Assessment of Violence Risk in Youth (SAVRY): Version 1.1.* Tampa, Florida: University of South Florida.

Borum, R., & Douglas, K. S. (2003). New directions in violence risk assessment, *Psychiatric Times.* Retrieved on September 18, 2005, from http://libproxy.nau.edu:2090/itw/infomark

Borum, R., Fein, R., Vossekuil, B., & Berglund, J. (1999). Threat assessment: Defining an approach for evaluating risk of targeted violence. *Behavioral Sciences and the Law, 17,* 323-337.

Borum, R., Otto, R., & Golding, S. (1993). Improving clinical judgment and decision making in forensic evaluation. *The Journal of Psychiatry and Law, 21,* 35-76.

Borum, R., Swartz, M., & Swanson, J. (1996). Assessing and managing violence risk in clinical practice. *Journal of Practical Psychiatry and Behavioral Health, 2,* 205-215.

Catchpole, R. E., & Gretton, H. M. (2003). The predicative validity of risk assessment with violent young offenders: A one-year examination of criminal outcome. *Criminal Justice and Behavior, 30,* 688-708.

Cottle, C. C., Lee, R. J., & Heilbrun, K. (2001). The prediction of criminal recidivism in juveniles. *Criminal Justice and Behavior, 28,* 367-394.

Cornell, D. G. (1990). Prior adjustment of violent juvenile offenders. *Law and Human Behavior, 14,* 569-577.

Cornell, D. G. (2004). Student threat assessment. In E. R. Gerler (Ed.), *Handbook of School Violence* (pp. 296-310). New York: Hawthorn Reference Press.

Dawes, R. M., Faust, D., & Meehl, P. E. (1989). Clinical versus actuarial judgment. *Science, 243,* 1668-1674.

DeVoe, J. F., Peter, K., Kaufman, P., Ruddy, S. A., Miller, A. K., Planty, M., et al. (2003). *Indicators of school crime and safety.* Washington, DC: U.S. Department of Education and U.S. Department of Justice.

DeVoe, J. F., Peter, K, Noonan, M., Snyder, T., & Baum, K (2005). *Indicators of school crime and safety.* Washington, DC: U.S. Department of Education and U.S. Department of Justice.

Douglas, K. S., Cox, D. N., & Webster, C. D., (1999). Violence risk assessment: Science and practice. *Legal and Criminological Psychology, 2,* 149-184.

Douglas, K. S., & Kropp, P. R. (2002). A prevention-based paradigm for violence risk assessment: Clinical and research applications. *Criminal Justice and Behavior, 29,* 617-658.

Douglas, K. S., & Ogloff, J. R. P. (2003a). Multiple facets of risk for violence: The impact of judgmental specificity on structured decisions about violence risk. *International Journal of Forensic Mental Health, 2,* 19-34.

Douglas, K. S., & Ogloff, J. R. P. (2003b). The impact of confidence on the accuracy of structured professional and actuarial violence risk judgments in a sample of forensic psychiatric patients. *Law and Human Behavior, 27*, 573-587.

Douglas, K. S., Ogloff, J. R. P., & Hart, S. D., (2003). Evaluation of a model of violence risk assessment among forensic psychiatric patients. *Psychiatric Services, 54*, 1372-1379.

Douglas, K. S., & Webster, C. D., (1999). Predicting violence in mentally and personality disordered individuals. In R. Roesch, S. D. Hart, & J. R. P. Ogloff (Eds.), *Psychology and Law: The State of the Discipline* (pp. 175-239). New York: Plenum Press.

Dwyer, K., & Osher, D. (2000). *Safeguarding Our Children: An Action Guide.* Washington, D.C.: U.S. Departments of Education and Justice, American Institutes for Reseach.

Dwyer, K., Osher, D., & Warger, C. (1998). *Early Warning, Timely Response: A Guide To Safe Schools.* Washington, D.C.: U.S. Department of Education.

Eaves, D., Douglas, K. S., Webster, C. D., Ogloff, J. R. P., & Hart, S. D. (2000). *Dangerous and long-term offenders: An assessment guide.* Vancouver, BC: The Mental Health, Law, and Policy Institute, Simon Fraser University.

Elliott, D. S. (1994). Serious violent offenders: Onset, developmental course, and termination-The American Society of Criminology 1993 presidential address. *Criminology, 32*, 1-21.

Farrington, D. P., (1989). Early predictors of adolescent aggression and adult violence. *Violence and Victims, 4*, 79-100.

Farrington, D. P. (1991). Childhood aggression and adult violence: Early precursors and later life outcomes. In D. Pepler & K. Rubin (Eds.), *The development and treatment of childhood aggression* (pp. 5-29). Hillsdale, NJ: Erlbaum.

Farrington, D. P. (1998). Predictors, causes, and correlates of male youth violence. In M. Tonry & M. H. Moore (Eds.), *Youth Violence* (pp. 421-475). Chicago: University of Chicago Press.

Farrington, D. P. (2000). Adolescent violence: Findings and implications from the Cambridge Study. In G. Boswell (Ed.), *Violent children and adolescents: Asking the question why* (pp. 19-35). London: Whurr.

Farrington, D. P. (2002). Multiple risk factors for multiple problem violent boys. In R. R. Corrado, R. Roesch, S. D. Hart, and J. K. Gierowski (Eds.), *Multi-Problem Violent Youth* (pp. 23-34). Washington, DC, IOS Press.

Farrington, D. P., & Loeber, R., (2000). Epidemiology of juvenile violence. *Child and Adolescent Psychiatric Clinics of North America, 9*, 733-747.

Fein, R. A., & Vossekuil, B., (1999). Assassination in the United States: An operational study of recent assassins, attackers, and near-lethal approachers. *Journal of Forensic Sciences, 44*, 321-333.

Fein, R. A., Vossekuil, B., Pollack, W. S., Borum, R., Modzeleski, W., & Reddy, M., (2002). The final report and findings of the Safe School Initiative: Implications for the prevention of school attacks in the United States. U.S. Department of Education, Office of Elementary and Secondary Education, Safe and Drug-Free Schools Program and U.S. Secret Service, National Threat Assessment Center, Washington DC.

Fitch, D. C. (2002). Analysis of common risk factors for violent behavior in Native American adolescents referred for residential treatment. Unpublished doctoral dissertation, Texas Southern University, Texas.

Forth, A. E., Kosson, D. S., & Hare, R. D. (2003). *The Psychopathy Checklist: Youth Version.* Toronto, Ontario, Canada: Multi-Health Systems.

Frick, P. J., Barry, C. T., & Bodin, S. D. (2000). Applying the concept of psychopathy to children: Implications for the assessment of antisocial youth. In C. B. Gacono (Ed.), *The clinical and forensic assessment of psychopathy: A practitioners guide* (pp. 3-24). Mahwah, NJ: Erlbaum.

Furlong, M., & Morrison, G. (1994). Introduction to miniseries: School violence and safety in perspective. *School Psychology Review, 23*, 139-150.

Furlong, M., & Morrison, G. (2000). The school in school violence: Definitions and facts. *Journal of Emotional & Behavioral Disorders, 8*, 71-81.

Gall, M. D., Gall, J. P., & Borg, W. R. (2003). Educational research: An introduction (7th ed.). White Plains, NY: Longman Publishers.

Grove, W., & Meehl, P. (1996). Comparative efficacy of informal (subjective, impressionistic) and formal (mechanical, algorithmic) prediction procedures: The clinical-statistical controversy. *Psychology, Public Policy, and Law, 2*, 293-323.

Grove, W. M., Zald, D. H., Lebow, B. S., Snitz, B. E., Nelson, C. (2000). Clinical versus mechanical prediction: A meta-analysis. *Psychological Assessment, 12*, 19-30.

Hanson, K. (1998). What we know about sex offender risk assessment. *Psychology, Public Policy, and Law, 4*, 50-72.

Harris, G. T., Rice, M. E., & Quinsey, V. L. (1993). Violent recidivism of mentally disordered offenders: The development of a statistical prediction instrument. *Criminal Justice and Behavior, 20*, 315-335.

Hart, S. D. (1998). The role of psychopath in assessing risk for violence: Conceptual and methodological issues. *Legal and Criminological Psychology, 3*, 121-137.

Hawkins, J., Herrenkohl, T., Farrington, D., Brewer, D., Catalano, R., & Harachi, T. (1998). A review of predictors of youth violence. In R. Loeber & D. Farrington (Eds.), *Serious and violent juvenile offenders: Risk factors and successful interventions* (pp. 106-146). Thousand Oaks, California: Sage Publications.

Hawkins, J. D., Herrenkohl, T. I., Farrington, D. P., Brewer, D., Catalano, R. F., Harachi, T. W., et al. (2000). Predictors of youth violence. *Juvenile Justice Bulletin*. Retrieved on January 28, 2006 from http://www.ncjrs.org/html/ ojjdp/jjbul2000_04_5/contents.html

Hoge, R. D., & Andrews, D. A. (1996). *Assessing the youthful offender: Issues and techniques.* New York: Plenum Press.

Hoge, R., & Andrews, D. (2002). *The Youth Level of Service/Case Management Inventory.* Toronto, Ontario, Canada: Multi-Health Systems.

James, B. (1994). School violence and the law: The search for suitable tools. *School Psychology Review, 23*, 190-203.

Koegl, C. J., Webster, C. D., Michel, M., & Augimeri, L. K. (2000). Coding raw data: Toward understanding raw life. *Child & Youth Care Forum, 29*, 229-246.

Kropp, P. R., Hart, S. D., Webster, C. D., & Eaves, D. (1999). *Manual for the Spousal Assault Risk Assessment Guide*, Third Edition. Toronto: Multi-Health Systems.

Larson, J. (1994). Violence prevention in the schools: A review of selected programs and procedures. *School Psychology Review, 23*, 151-164.

Leech, N. L., Barrett, H. D., & Morgan, G. A. (2005). *SPSS for intermediate statistics: Use and interpretation* (2nd ed.). Mahwah, NJ: Lawrence Erlbaum Associates, Publishers.

Levene, K. S., Augimeri, L. K., Pepler, D. J., Walsh, M. M., Webster, C. D., & Koegl, C. J. (2001). *Early Assessment Risk List for Girls: EARL-21G, Version 1, consultation edition.* Toronto, Canada: Earlscourt Child and Family Centre.

Lipsey, M. W., & Derzon, J. H. (1998). Predictors of violent or serious delinquency in adolescence and early adulthood. In R. Loeber. & D. P. Farrington (Eds.), *Serious & Violent Juvenile Offenders: Risk factors and successful interventions* (pp. 87-106). Thousand Oaks, California: Sage Publications.

Loeber, R., Farrington, D. P., & Waschbusch, D. A. (1998). Serious and violent juvenile offenders. In R. Loeber. & D. P. Farrington (Eds.), *Serious & Violent Juvenile Offenders: Risk factors and successful interventions* (pp. 13-29). Thousand Oaks, California: Sage Publications.

Loeber, R., Farrington, D. P., Stouthamer-Loeber, M., Moffitt, T. E., & Caspi, A. (2001). The development of male offending: Key findings from the first decade of the Pittsburgh Youth Study. In B. Ray (Ed.), *Children and the Law: The Essential Readings* (pp. 336-378). Malden, MA: Blackwell Publishers.

Martin, R. C. (2001). Zero tolerance policy. *American Bar Association Journal.* Retrieved December 3, 2005, from www.abanet.org/crimjust/juvjus/zerotolreport.html

McEachran, A. (2001). The predictive validity of the PCL:YV and the SAVRY in a population of adolescent offenders. Unpublished master's thesis, Simon Fraser University, Canada.

McGraw, K. O., & Wong, S. P. (1996). Forming inferences about some intraclass correlation coefficients. *Psychological Methods, 1,* 30-46.

Melton, G., Petrila, J., Poythress, N., & Slobogin, C. (1997). *Psychological evaluations for the courts: A handbook for mental health professionals and lawyers* (2nd ed.). New York: Guilford Press.

Miller, G. (1994). School violence mini-series: Impressions and implications. *School Psychology Review, 23,* 257-261.

Monahan, J. (1981). *Predicting violent behavior: An assessment of clinical techniques.* Beverly Hills, California: Sage Publications.

Monahan, J. (1996). Violence prediction: The last 20 years and the next 20 years. *Criminal Justice and Behavior, 23,* 107-120.

Monahan, J. (1997). Actuarial support for the clinical assessment of violence risk. *International Review of Psychiatry, 9,* 167-169.

Monahan, J., & Steadman, H. J. (1994). *Violence and mental disorder: Developments in risk assessment.* Chicago: The University of Chicago Press.

Monahan, J., & Steadman, H. (2001). Violence risk assessment: A quarter century of research. In L. Frost & R. Bonnie (Eds.), *The evolution of mental health law* (pp. 195-211). Washington, DC: American Psychological Association.

Monahan, J., Steadman, H. J., Silver, E., Appelbaum, P. S., Robbins, P. C., Mulvey, E. P., et al. (2001). *Rethinking risk assessment: The MacArthur study of mental disorder and violence.* New York: Oxford University Press.

Morrison, G. M., Furlong, M. J., & Morrison, R. L. (1994). School violence to school safety: Reframing the issue for school psychologists. *School Psychology Review, 23,* 236-256.

Mossman, D. (1994). Assessing predictions of violence: Being accurate about accuracy. *Journal of Consulting and Clinical Psychology, 62,* 783-794.

Otto, R. (1992). The prediction of dangerous behavior: A review and analysis of 'second generation' research. *Forensic Reports, 5,* 103-133.

Otto, R. (2000). Assessing and managing violence risk in outpatient settings. *Journal of Clinical Psychology, 56,* 1239-1262.

Parker, J., & Asher, S. (1987). Peer relations and later personal adjustment: Are low accepted children at risk? *Psychological Bulletin, 102,* 357-389.

Poland, S. (1994). The role of school crisis intervention teams to prevent and reduce school violence trauma. *School Psychology Review, 23,* 175-189.

Reddy, M., Borum, R., Berglund, J., Vossekuil, B., Fein, R., & Modzeleski, W. (2001). Evaluating risk for targeted violence in schools: Comparing risk assessment, threat assessment, and other approaches. *Psychology in the Schools, 38,* 157-172.

Skiba, R., & Peterson, R. (1999a). The dark side of zero tolerance: Can punishment lead to safe schools? *Phi Delta Kappan, 80,* 372–379.

Skiba, R., & Peterson, R. (1999b). Zap zero tolerance. *Education Digest, 64,* 24-31.

Small, M., & Dressler-Tetrick, K. (2001). School violence: An overview. *Juvenile Justice, 8,* 3-12.

Snyder, H. N. (2004). Juvenile arrests 2002. *Juvenile Justice Bulletin.* Retrieved January 5, 2006, from http://www.ncjrs.gov/pdffiles1/ojjdp/204608.pdf

Soriano, M., Soriano, F. I., & Jimenez, E. (1994). School violence among culturally diverse populations: Sociocultural and institutional considerations. *School Psychology Review, 23*, 216-235.

Swets, J. A. (1996). *Signal detection theory and ROC analysis in psychological and diagnostics: Collected papers*. New Jersey: Lawrence Erlbaum Associates.

Swets, J. A., Dawes, R. M., & Monahan, J. (2000). Psychological science can improve diagnostic decisions. *Psychological Science in the Public Interest*, 1-26.

Tabachnick, B., & Fidell, L. (2007). *Using multivariate statistics* (5th ed.). Needham Heights, California: Allyn and Bacon.

Tebo, M. G. (2000). Zero tolerance, zero sense. *American Bar Association Journal*. Retrieved December 3, 2005, from www.abanet.org/crimjust/juvjus/04FZERO.html

University of South Florida (n.d.). *SAVRY: Structured Assessment of Violence Risk in Youth*. Retrieved November 27, 2005, from http://www.fmhi.usf.edu/mhlp/savry/SAVRY_Research.htm

Vossekuil, B., Fein, R., Reddy, M., Borum, R., & Modzeleski, W. (2002). *The final report and findings of the safe school initiative: Implications for the prevention of school attacks in the United States*. Washington, D.C.: U.S. Department of Education, Office of Elementary and Secondary Education, Safe and Drug Free Schools Program and U.S. Secret Service, National Threat Assessment Center.

Webster, C. D., Douglas, K. S., Eaves, D., & Hart, S. D., (1997). Assessing risk of violence to others. In C. D. Webster & M. Jackson (Eds.), *Impulsivity: Theory, Assessment, & Treatment* (pp. 251-277). New York: Guilford.

APPENDICES

Appendix A

Structured Assessment of Violence Risk in Youth:
Basic Coding Sheet
Adapted from Bartel, Borum, and Forth, 2000

Name/ID: _____

DOB: _____ Age: _____

Evaluator: _____

Historical Risk Factors		Rating 1-2-3-X	Critical Item	Location in File
1.	History of Violence			
2.	History of Non-Violent Offending			
3.	Early Initiation of Violence			
4.	Past Supervision/Intervention Failures			
5.	History of Self-Harm or Suicide Attempts			
6.	Exposure to Violence in the Home			
7.	Childhood History of Maltreatment			
8.	Parental/Caregiver Criminality			
9.	Early Caregiver Disruption			
10.	Poor School Achievement			

Social/Contextual Risk Factors		Rating 1-2-3-X	Critical Item	Location in File
11.	Peer Delinquency			
12.	Peer Rejection			
13.	Stress and Poor Coping			
14.	Poor Parental Management			
15.	Lack of Personal/Social Support			
16.	Community Disorganization			

Individual/Clinical Risk Factors		Rating 1-2-3-X	Critical Item	Location in File
17.	Negative Attitudes			
18.	Risk Taking/Impulsivity			
19.	Substance Use Difficulties			
20.	Anger Management Problems			
21.	Low Empathy/Remorse			
22.	Attention Deficit/Hyperactivity Difficulties			
23.	Poor Compliance			
24.	Low Interest/Commitment to School			

Appendix A, continued

SAVRY Coding Sheet

Protective Factors		Rating 0-1-X	Critical Item	Location in File
P1.	Prosocial Involvement			
P2.	Strong Social Support			
P3.	Strong Attachments and Bonds			
P4.	Positive Attitude Towards Intervention and Authority			
P5.	Strong Commitment to School			
P6.	Resilient Personality Traits			

Summary Rating of Risk			
Rating of Risk	Low	Moderate	High

Appendix B

Demographic Coding Form
Page 1
Complete using information contained within the cumulative file.

CASE NUMBER _____   DATE COMPLETED _____

Gender: Male   Female

Current Academic Grade: 5   6   7   8   9   10   11   12

Date of Birth: _____

Ethnicity: ___Caucasian;
                  ___Hispanic;
                  ___African American;
                  ___Asian;
                  ___Native American;
                  ___Middle Eastern;
                  ___Other

Program Entry Date: _____   **Exit Date**:   _____

Grade Point Average (adjusted): <1.5   1.6-2.0   2.0-3.0   3.0-3.5   3.5-4.0

Special Education Eligibility Area(s):   Primary: _____

                                         Other: _____

                                         Other: _____

                                         Other: _____

DSM-IV Diagnosis: _____

Fee and Reduced Lunch: YES   NO

Household: ___dual parent
                  ___single parent
                  ___grandparent
                  ___foster care
                  ___group home
                  ___relative (aunt, uncle, sibling)

Demographic Coding Form
Page 2
Complete using information contained within the cumulative file.

Truancy (#): _____

Absences (#): _____

Home Language: _____

Grade Retention: YES   NO

Educationally based services: ____   Speech

                                       ____   OT

                                       ____   PT

                                       ____   Counseling

                                       ____   Nursing

                                       ____   Adaptive P.E.

                                       ____   Other _____

Appendix C

File Review

CUMULATIVE FILE (1.00)

Item	General Description
Court report (1.1)	Custody and parental rights
Note from parent (1.2)	Permission to pick up child
Pupil registration form (1.3)	Demographic information – child and family
Permission slip (1.4)	Granting involvement in community based instruction
Birth Certificate (1.5)	Date, state, and county of birth
Screening for handicapping condition (1.6)	Screening form for special education needs including areas of concern (vision, hearing, social/emotional/behavioral, academic, psychomotor)
Withdrawal Form (1.7)	Date of withdrawal and reason
Request for release of records (1.8)	From private community based provider
Attorney's records (1.9)	Regarding custody case and restraining order
Progress report (1.10)	Summative grading per semester and teacher comments by grade level
Calendar Card (1.11)	Days absent from school
Immunization Record (1.12)	Date and nature of immunization
Photography/Name release (1.13)	Parent permission to release name and take photo
Electronic information system user (1.14)	Parent permission to use internet at school
Attendance and Truancy Procedures (1.15)	Notification signed by parent
Residency Form (1.16)	Addresses McKinney-Vento Assistance Act

CUMULATIVE FILE (1.00), continued

Item	General Description
Staff documentation (1.17)	Record and date of phone conversation with Parent
Home language survey (1.18)	First language spoken by student, language at home, and student's primary language
Records from previous school (1.19)	Attendance, grades, proof of residence

INTERVENTION FILE (2.00)

Item	General Description
Point sheets (2.1)	Daily behavior records
Referral Consequence form (2.2)	Record of student's processing of skill
One to one Intervention (2.3)	Record of date and nature of incident necessitating student being sent from classroom to intervention room to process

DISCIPLINARY FILE (3.00)

Item	General Description
In-school suspensions (3.1)	Date, duration, and nature of incident
Out of school suspensions (3.2)	Date, duration, and nature of incident

ARREST HISTORY FILE (4.00)

Item	General Description
Arrests made at school (4.1)	Date, charge, nature of incident
Probation officer (4.2)	Name, contact information
General information (4.3)	Pending court dates, warrants, arrests outside of school (partial list), court reports

INDIVIDUAL EDUCATION PLAN FILE (5.00)

Item	General Description
Initial placement form (5.1)	Date of enrollment at school
Parent conference request (5.2)	Notice of meeting, who attends, and purpose
IEP	
Cover page (5.3)	Demographics, placement, eligibility, vision/hearing, duration of IEP, signatures of participants
Conference report (5.4)	Written summary of meeting, parent input
Present levels of educational Performance (5.5)	Strengths and weaknesses, needs based summary
Annual Goal (5.6)	Goal and objective to be measured
Services to be provided (5.7)	Nature, dates, where, and who (e.g., nursing, counseling, speech therapy, physical therapy, transportation, etc.)
Program Adaptations (5.8)	Accommodations and modifications, Extended school year
Consideration of special factors (5.9)	Need for (behavior plan, assistive technology, transition services, limited English proficiency, blind, deaf), participation in state or district norm referenced tests, privately placed students, consideration of effects of placement on child.
Prior Written Notice (5.10)	Action taken or not take and reason
Closed out goals (annual) (5.11)	Previous goals with outcomes noted
Educational plan report (5.12)	Private residential facility, progress noted (academic/behavioral)

Appendix C, continued
File Review

PSYCHO-EDUCATIONAL FILE (6.00)

Item	General Description
Multidisciplinary Evaluation Team (6.1)	Documentation of information considered and eligibility decisions
Eligibility forms (6.2)	Specific criteria met for each area of Eligibility
Review of existing data (6.3)	Information reviewed as part of evaluation
Observation (in-class) (6.4)	Observation of behaviors in class and other Settings
Functional Behavioral Assessments (6.5)	Behavioral analysis addressing function of problematic behavior as well as identifying possible replacement behaviors
Therapy services (private) (6.6)	Therapeutic interventions implemented outside of school by private providers
Psychiatric Evaluation Report (6.7)	Presenting problem, history of substance use, past psychiatric history, family psychiatric history, developmental history, medical history, social history, mental status examination, assessment, diagnoses, plan/recommendation
Neuropsychological Evaluation (6.8)	Interview with parent and student, background information summary, test results, behavioral observations, attention/concentration/cognitive processing speed, perceptual motor skills, learning and memory, intelligence and executive functioning, personality test results, impressions and comments, recommendations

Appendix C, continued
File Review

PSYCHO-EDUCATIONAL FILE (6.00), continued

Item	General Description
Psycho-educational Evaluation (6.9)	Reason for referral, sources of information, background information, developmental history, behavioral observations, determination of disadvantages, assessment accommodation, test instruments, interpretation of cognitive ability, academic achievement, social emotional functioning, adaptive behavior, social skills, visual-motor processing, summary of eligibility, and recommendations
Speech Language Evaluation (6.10)	Reason for referral, sources of information, background information, developmental history, behavioral observations, test instruments, interpretation, summary of eligibility, recommendations
Physical Therapy Evaluation (6.11)	Reason for referral, sources of information, background information, developmental history, behavioral observations, assessment procedures, interpretation, summary of eligibility, recommendations
Occupational Therapy Evaluation (6.12)	Reason for referral, sources of information, background information, developmental history, behavioral observations, assessment procedures, interpretation, summary of eligibility, recommendations

This information was generated based upon review of a student's files. The sources of information within each student's files may vary in terms of content and items included. However, at minimum, each student will have these files that contain an Individual Education Plan, Psycho-educational Evaluation(s), academic history, attendance, and disciplinary history.

Appendix D

Violence Coding Sheet
Criterion Variable
page 1

CASE NUMBER _____   DATE _____

The criterion variable, **violent acts** perpetrated during the most recent academic year sampled, for this study will be operationally defined in accordance with the Structured Assessment of Violence Risk in Youth (SAVRY; Borum, Bartel, & Forth, 2003) manual as follows:

4. *"A violent act will be defined as an act of battery or physical violence that is sufficiently severe to cause injury to another person or persons (i.e., cuts, bruises, broken bones, death, etc.), regardless of whether injury actually occurs; any act of sexual assault; or a threat made with a weapon in hand"* (p. 15).

5. These acts should be of sufficient severity that criminal charges either did, or could have, resulted.

Non-violent offending will also be collected using this form. For the purposes of this study, frequency of non-violent offending will be collected for the same period of time as the criterion variable. Consistent with the SAVRY definition, non-offending will be defined as follows:

A) *Any criminal or delinquent activity that does not involve battery such as theft, burglary, drug sales, and serious destruction of property;*

B) Regardless of whether it resulted in formal criminal charge or conviction.

For the purposes of this study, each violent act, as defined above, will be independent and counted only once toward the Total Behavioral Acts.

Number of acts that meet the criteria for:	Violent offending	Nonviolent offending
1) Discipline Referrals as documented in file	_____	_____
2) Intervention records as documented in file	_____	_____
3) Arrest history as documented in file	_____	_____
TOTAL Behavioral Acts	_____	_____

Appendix D, continued

Violence Coding Sheet
Criterion Variable
page 2

Violent offending

Source	Date	Nature of incident

Appendix D, continued

Violence Coding Sheet
Criterion Variable
page 3

Non-violent offending

Source	Date	Nature of incident

Wissenschaftlicher Buchverlag bietet

kostenfreie

Publikation

von

wissenschaftlichen Arbeiten

Diplomarbeiten, Magisterarbeiten, Master und Bachelor Theses
sowie Dissertationen, Habilitationen und wissenschaftliche Monographien

Sie verfügen über eine wissenschaftliche Abschlußarbeit zu aktuellen oder zeitlosen
Fragestellungen, die hohen inhaltlichen und formalen Ansprüchen genügt,
und haben **Interesse an einer honorarvergüteten Publikation**?

Dann senden Sie bitte erste Informationen über Ihre Arbeit per Email
an info@vdm-verlag.de. Unser Außenlektorat meldet sich umgehend bei Ihnen.

VDM Verlag Dr. Müller Aktiengesellschaft & Co. KG
Dudweiler Landstraße 125a
D - 66123 Saarbrücken

www.vdm-verlag.de

Printed by
Schaltungsdienst Lange o.H.G., Berlin